JERKS AT WORK

EDITED AND TYPESET BY GINA TALUCCI

Cover design by Lu Rossman / Digi Dog Design

Printed in the U.S.A. by Book-mart Press

To order this title, please call toll-free 1-800-CAREER-1 (NJ and Canada: 201-848-0310) to order using VISA or MasterCard, or for further information on books from Career Press.

CAREER
PRESS

The Career Press, Inc., 3 Tice Road, PO Box 687,
Franklin Lakes, NJ 07417
www.careerpress.com

Library of Congress Cataloging-in-Publication Data

Lloyd, Kenneth L.
Jerks at work : how to deal with people problems and problem people / by Ken Lloyd.—[2nd ed.]
p. cm.
Includes index.
ISBN 1-56414-852-1 (paper)
1. Problem employees. 2. Interpersonal relationships. I. Title.

HF5549.5.E42L58 2005
658.3ʹ045--dc22

2005051326

How to Deal With People Problems and Problem People

By Ken Lloyd, Ph.D.

Nationally Syndicated Columnist

CAREER
PRESS
Franklin Lakes, N.J.

This is dedicated to
Roberta, Jessica, Stacey, and Josh—
and so am I.

Acknowledgments

As was the case in the first edition of this book, there are, again, many people who deserve thanks, credit, and appreciation for helping to bring this new edition of *Jerks at Work* to life. And once again, there is not a jerk among them.

During the past 10 years that my column has been running in the *Los Angeles Daily News,* and numerous other papers across the United States, I have received all sorts of e-mails, letters, and phone calls from readers with as broad a range of workplace questions as one can imagine. Without these readers, this book would not exist, so I offer them great thanks for taking the time to read my columns and for contacting me. I greatly appreciate the confidence they have placed in my approach to dealing with people problems and problem people.

Before the first edition of *Jerks at Work* was ever on the drawing board, several readers had inquired about the possibility of me placing my columns in a book. Their encouragement played a key role in bringing the original book to life. During the recent years, more readers inquired about the possibility of a sequel. This new edition is due, in great part, to their encouragement. So, I actually offer double thanks to my readers.

I also thank the staff and leadership at the *Los Angeles Daily News* for their support of my column. It has been a pleasure to work with David Butler, the editor, along with the friendly, responsive, and professional staff.

There are several people at Career Press who, once again, literally could not have been more helpful. For all of the time, energy, creativity, and support that they put into this project, I thank publisher Ron Fry, Mike Lewis, Gina Talucci, Kate Henches, and all other members of the outstanding Career Press team.

Thanks also to the entire team at the *New York Times* syndicate for their support of my column. In this regard, I offer very special thanks to a couple of very special editors: Denise Balle and Yvette Benedek.

And finally, I thank my own outstanding editor, library director, and best friend, Roberta Winston Lloyd, whose insight, understanding, and patience on this project and on all others, know no limits. I also thank Jessica, Stacey, and Josh for letting me do my homework.

Table of Contents

Introduction

As was the case in the first edition of *Jerks at Work*, this book answers real questions, from real people, about real jerks at work. However, in the more than years since the first edition was published, there have been some significant changes in the workplace that have led to entirely new realms of jerk-like behavior. For example, in the book's first edition, words such as "bullies," "online," and "cell phone," were not even in the index. In this book, there are chapters on each, and much more.

This book provides steps, tools, and strategies to handle the broad and ever-expanding range of jerk-like behaviors in the workplace. By focusing on real-world questions about jerks at work, the book provides answers that are neither hypothetical nor theoretical. Rather, each delves into the causes and outcomes of the problematic behaviors and then presents proven hands-on techniques to deal with them.

Every question was originally mailed, e-mailed, or telephoned to my weekly workplace advice column that is syndicated by the *New York Times* syndicate. The column has run in the *Los Angeles Daily News* for 10 years, as well as many other newspapers across the United States.

Through the years, the column has transformed from being a source of answers for garden variety questions (such as an explanation of the difference between exempt and non-exempt employees) into a clearinghouse for jerk-related questions. Questions today are almost exclusively focused on how to deal with ridiculous behaviors by jerks as managers, jerks as supervisors, jerks as coworkers, jerks as subordinates, jerks as customers, jerks as friends, jerks as trainers, jerks in the family business, and jerks just about anywhere else in the world of work.

In addition, with each passing year, there are more and more letters on workplace behaviors that are increasingly ridiculous. To further prove this point, there is another new chapter that provides a sampling of the past five years' most absolutely outrageous workplace behaviors, antics, policies, and expectations. For example, how about a company with a travel policy that requires employees to share accommodations co-ed?

The reality is that jerks can be present in any and all aspects of work. They can put their imprint on hiring, training, company policies, promotions, e-mail, salaries, benefits, recognition, and just about anything else that goes on in an organization. They can emerge at any job level, from the most senior ownership position all the way to an entry-level position, and even to job applicants themselves. And regardless of title or position, they are always on the lookout for ways to demonstrate their wares. This means that all others must be wary.

Even one jerk in an organization can be a source of problems that extend far beyond his or her domain. In fact, a jerk's actions can create problems not only for those who work in the same area, but also for entire departments and even the organization at large. And that's just one jerk, which means that the problems expand exponentially with each additional jerk.

There is no instant, automatic, or generic strategy to deal with every card-carrying jerk and the problems he or she creates. Rather, jerks and the messes they make are best approached on an individual basis. With insight into what makes the jerk tick, plus a full comprehension of the damage they caused, it is much easier to take highly effective and productive action. There now are time-tested strategies as well as new cutting-edge approaches to dealing with jerks at work. If you are looking for those strategies and approaches, you picked the right book.

Chapter 1

Preemployment Problems

During every stage of the preemployment process, there are endless opportunities for jerks on both sides of the desk to demonstrate ill-conceived antics and poorly chosen behaviors.

Employers can ask inappropriate questions, use ridiculous tests, rely on useless data, and generally treat an applicant in much the same way they do a paperclip; there are plenty of them around, they can be easily bent and twisted, their individual value is minimal, and they can be tossed out without any misgivings. This type of treatment makes absolutely no sense because numerous studies continue to find that one of the key factors in determining whether an applicant ultimately accepts or rejects a job offer is the way that he or she is treated during the screening process.

Many interviewers fail to comprehend the fact that the way a company treats its job applicants is a clear indicator of the way it treats people in general. There are far too many situations where preemployment treatment is best described (and worst described) as shabby, thoughtless, rude, and clearly unprofessional.

At the same time, there are plenty of applicants who are living proof that there are some heavy-duty jerks populating the labor market. Many of these applicants do not understand that a job interview is actually a sales presentation, and the objective is to build trust, understand the interviewer's needs, and then provide compelling proof that such needs will be more than met by making a job offer.

There are applicants who take themselves out of the running before the race even starts, such as creating bogus resumes. Other outrageous behaviors during the interviews and afterwards also toss them quickly into the corporate trash bin.

In spite of it all, there are still plenty of jerks who are doing the screening, along with plenty of jerks who are being screened. This means that there are occasions where both interviewer and interviewee are scoring high on the jerk scale. In such scenarios, the wrong people are being hired for the wrong jobs in the wrong companies by the wrong individuals.

The never-ending resume

Q. My resume is four pages long. Some people tell me I am violating one of the cardinal rules about applying for a job, and others say it is not a problem. Is a four page resume too long?

A. When your resume is four pages long, you should say so long to it. There is no hard and fast rule about resume length, but when a resume exceeds two pages, the chances of it getting a full reading diminish quickly.

Your resume is an advertisement for you. Think of the advertisements that you actually read. Are they filled with verbiage from one end to the other, or are they succinct and clear? In addition, a long resume can send some mixed messages about you. For example, some employers might think you are a bit egocentric, while others might assume that you did not devote enough time to developing a more focused resume. As Mark Twain said, "I didn't have time to write a short letter, so I wrote a long one instead."

Do a line-by-line review of your resume, asking yourself if each detail truly provides information that is relevant to the position and helps you stand out from other applicants.

Some resumes are initially scanned by computers that look for key words and phrases that relate to the job. However, at some point, a human is going to get your resume, and if it reads like a history book, you are likely to be history.

A counselor's ridiculous counsel

Q. I went to see an employment counselor and he suggested that I "forget about" three brief jobs and take them off my resume. He said it is very competitive out there, and these jobs will hurt my chances of even getting an interview. Should I follow this advice?

A. When an employment counselor suggests that you forget about a few jobs, a better suggestion is to forget about him. This employment counselor is absolutely correct in telling you that the labor market is very competitive, but there is nothing correct in telling you to lie in order to get an interview.

In the first place, it is simply wrong to lie. If that is not reason enough, you should also remember that as part of the hiring process, you certify that all of the information you are providing is true, and if any of it has been willfully falsified, you will be removed from consideration or terminated in the event that you are hired.

Many employers today are taking their time to check out applicants very carefully, including references from previous jobs. If one of those references mentions a company that you "forgot about," you're finished.

By focusing more on what is in your career, and less on what a counselor may be telling you to conceal, you will have a better chance of finding and keeping the job you want.

A test or a toy?

Q. We've had some turnover among new hires, and my manager suggested I use a five-minute personality test to help me hire new staff. He said he completed the test and it described him perfectly. I'm not real comfortable using it. What's your opinion of this type of test?

A. The best thing that can be said about a five-minute personality test is that it takes five minutes to complete. These tests have absolutely no place in the hiring process. They are essentially parlor games, and, as such, they belong in the game room.

Preemployment testing can be highly valuable in screening applicants. However, selection, administration, and interpretation of any test is serious business and calls for expertise in such areas as test validation, Equal Employment Opportunity guidelines, adverse impact, job-relatedness of the questions, and much more.

When employers use preemployment tests that ignore professional standards, they subject themselves to major legal exposure, as well as the loss of highly qualified applicants who are annoyed or offended by the tests themselves.

As for the five-minute test describing your boss "perfectly," all it is actually doing is parroting back what he said. For example, if he says that he is friendly, the test will spout that back to him. But what if he is not really friendly at all, but simply responded that way because that is how he thinks he is or how he wants to be seen? A real personality test would catch this.

Instead of wasting five minutes on this test, spend five extra minutes on the applicant's work experience.

Forget me? Forget you!

Q. I had an appointment for a job interview, and I called in the morning to confirm it. When I got to the company, a secretary told me that the interview was cancelled because the person who was supposed to interview me had to go to a meeting. Now whenever I call back, I cannot get an interview date. Any suggestions?

A. There's only one suggestion in this situation: forget about this company. When they cancelled the interview with you, they should have taken extra steps to reschedule it as soon as possible. However, the only steps they have taken are to move further away from you.

A job interview can be legitimately cancelled at the last minute, as any number of business emergencies may arise. But there is nothing legitimate about the runaround that the company is now giving you.

Their action provides several important pieces of data. In the first place, it gives you valuable insight into the way they treat people in general.

There is some question about their ability to keep commitments, and they do not seem to have much concern for goodwill.

Perhaps the strongest message is that they are not interested in you. No matter what may have caused them to pass on you, this could be one of the real breaks in your career.

Don't pencil it in

Q. I am applying for a sales job and the interviewer picked up a pencil and asked me to sell it to her. I have been successfully selling for eight years, and that's the proof of my sales ability. Is this what salespeople have to do now?

A. Fortunately, most interviewers for sales jobs expect applicants to sell themselves, not pencils. Perhaps if you were applying for a job at a pencil company or door-to-door sales where you get one quick shot at a prospect, this type of question would be appropriate. But even if that were the case, there are far better predictors of success than this contrived interaction that is so far removed from the real world of selling.

This simplistic approach tells the interviewer nothing about an applicant's ability to plan a sales session, identify the prospect's needs, move sales through the pipeline, sell intangibles, or provide service and support. In other words, the exercise provides no meaningful data to help the interviewer make a successful hiring decision.

Selling today has become far more sophisticated. Sales professionals are better educated and trained, and a growing number of businesses are using high-tech customer relationship management (CRM) solutions to organize and track every step of the sales process.

Excellent salespeople can get jobs in just about any economic conditions, and companies can lose some excellent candidates by playing games with them. The best way to predict success of a salesperson is to review his or her sales history, rather than watching him or her pretend to sell a pencil.

The wrong calls

Q. I was in a job interview and the interviewer took a personal phone call. He hardly apologized afterwards, and I felt insulted and rather foolish. I never got a call back from him, even though I followed up with a letter and phone calls. I am still upset by this treatment, and I wonder if there is anything I should do now.

A. Not to get personal, but an interviewer who takes a personal call during a job interview should be required to sit at the children's table in the company dining room.

The best step to take now is to try to forget about the shabby treatment you received at this company and focus your energy and efforts on finding the right job at the right company. When interviewers treat an applicant poorly, the applicant should interpret it as a major red flag about the company itself.

However, if you absolutely want to work for this company and you just cannot get over what happened, you have nothing to lose by calling the interviewer's boss, describing the interview, and asking if other options are available. The worst outcome is that you will not be offered a job that was not being offered in the first place.

In today's labor market, there's no question that some companies are treating job applicants poorly. However, economies run in cycles, and when things turn around, companies that have developed a reputation for treating an applicant as a nobody may well find that nobody wants to work for them.

What you see isn't what you get

Q. We interviewed an individual whom we thought was the ideal candidate. His skills were just what we were looking for, and the chemistry seemed great. Now that he has been on board for a few weeks, I think we made a big mistake. He is totally different from the friendly and easy-going person we interviewed. What happened here?

A. When you hire a hopeful applicant, only to see him turn into a hopeless employee, any number of problems could have occurred. In the first place, there is no perfect hiring system. Even if you are using the most sophisticated hiring techniques, all you will be doing is improving the probability of making a successful hire. Hiring errors are still going to occur.

This situation also signals that it may be worthwhile to review your hiring system. This can include updating the job description, making sure the interview process is structured and job related, and using appropriate steps to take references. During the interview, it is not particularly difficult to determine if the applicant has the skills to get the job done, while it is a more complex matter to predict if he or she has the motivation, persistence, and interpersonal skills to do so effectively. The best way to determine this is to develop a very clear picture of this person's work history.

At the same time, it will also be helpful to look at the level of support and guidance that new employees are receiving in your company. Is it possible that the *applicant* thought he was joining a friendly and easy-going company, but found something totally different?

Seeing eye to eye

Q. I just interviewed a young man for a job with our company, and he seems to be well qualified. However, I was bothered by his failure to look me in the eye when he answered a question. I get the feeling that people who do that are not telling the truth. Some of my employees tell me that I am way off base on this. Are they right?

A. Although you do not see eye to eye with your employees on this matter, they are absolutely right. There is no evidence that people who do not maintain eye contact are lying.

There are all sorts of biases, preconceptions, and stereotypes about people that can prevent an interviewer from getting an accurate picture of a job applicant. If you allow any of them to get in your way, you will significantly decrease your chances of making a successful and equitable hiring decision.

After all, there is no rule that prescribes how much an interviewee is supposed to look into the eyes of the interviewer. While some how-to books advise applicants to glance occasionally into the interviewer's eyes, and not to stare, the best advice for interviewees is to be themselves, lest they sell a product that they cannot deliver.

At the same time, there is an interesting aspect of eye contact that may be playing a role here. In some cultures, it is considered to be rather impolite to look into the eyes of another. This means that you may be looking at another aspect of diversity in the work force. And as numerous studies have already found, employee diversity is clearly contributing to increases in organizational effectiveness, innovation, and goal attainment.

The best way to approach any job applicant is with an open mind, and your willingness to think further about the issue of eye contact demonstrates that you have one. From this point, you should be pleased to have found an applicant whom you believe is well-qualified. The best step is to meet with him again to further discuss his work history and to ask him some work-sample questions to further assess his expertise. If this is a dishonest individual, it will be reflected far more clearly in his career path than in his eyes.

Don't call me; I won't call you

Q. I asked a friend to help me find a job, so he called a friend of his at a large telecom company. I called this person six times and never received so much as a call back saying "no." Is this rudeness today's attitude or "company policy"?

A. It appears that the practice of selectively ignoring phone messages that was once reserved for Hollywood execs has now become the hallmark of staffers at almost any company in America. One of the most common complaints being voiced by today's job seekers is having their phone messages and inquiries ignored.

This treatment makes job seekers feel that they are being personally ignored, and this hurts. If it happens enough times, it does not take long before their self-esteem, self-image, and confidence start to suffer.

Many people today only return phone calls if the caller is either more powerful or has something that the recipient needs. Other than that, phone calls are ignored unless the recipient is feeling momentarily benevolent. It would be difficult to find any company policy that encourages employees to act this way. Such a policy would not do much in terms of building internal or external goodwill.

Fortunately, there still are some staffers out there who understand that returning phone calls makes sense from a business standpoint as well as a personal standpoint. And for those individuals who persist in selectively ignoring incoming calls, they should understand that in this economy, some day the bell may toll for them.

Picky, picky

Q. We just interviewed an excellent applicant for a high level sales position. After the interview, we went to lunch and I was shocked when he stuck a toothpick in his mouth on the way out of the restaurant. His whole appearance changed, and I think my opinion of him changed, too. Do you think this is acceptable professional behavior?

A. If you found an outstanding candidate for a high level sales position and your only complaint is about a toothpick, you are being too picky. Obviously, if he went through a whole oral hygiene procedure, that is another matter.

There are people at all job levels who find it comforting to pop in a toothpick after a meal. Because you are screening a salesperson, he is probably a fairly oral fellow, and a toothpick may be gratifying some of these needs.

Presumably he has established a highly successful track record, so it does not appear that a toothpick has created any problems in the past. In fact, perhaps that toothpick has even helped him sell.

Instead of worrying about what he puts in his mouth, try to focus on what comes out of it, namely his ability to communicate persuasively. As an excellent salesperson, he is conditioned to be sensitive to any behaviors that interfere with his ability to close sales. If he finds that his customers don't like the toothpick, he'll pick up the cue and not the toothpick.

A lie is a lie

Q. We recently interviewed a young applicant who seemed perfect. When we took references, we found discrepancies regarding his job titles, responsibilities, and employment dates. When we asked him about this, he said lots of young people today have to embellish their backgrounds to get a job, and he already showed us he has the skills. He probably does, but I'm wondering if we should take him out of the running.

A. There is indeed evidence that some young people are resorting to "embellishment" and worse in order to get past the resume scanners and into a job. However, the fact that this is occurring does not make it right.

You can certainly think of situations in business today where various executives were engaging in ethically questionable behaviors, and their fellow employees used such behaviors as justification for their own questionable actions. That's just the kind of person you will be hiring if you go with this individual.

Are you at all troubled by the fact that he looked you in the eye and lied? If you hire him, what are you going to think when he is working on a critical project and looks at you the same way and describes how the project is going? Because of his antics in the hiring process, you are most likely going to have doubts whenever you meet with him.

You should leave him in the labor pool and fish around for some of the truly terrific applicants of all ages who are out there.

War of the words

Q. I interviewed an applicant who made some inappropriate comments about females. Because I am a male, I guess he thought he could say them to me. I told him his remarks are wrong and he is out of touch with reality. An argument ensued before the interview ended. When I told my manager, he said I should never get into an argument with an applicant, no matter what the applicant says. I disagree. What do you think?

A. Your manager is arguably right. When you interview an applicant who makes inappropriate comments, it is equally inappropriate for you to get into verbal fisticuffs. Your job is to learn about applicants, not change them.

There is an easy way to deal with applicants who make sexist comments during a job interview. You can cut these remarks short by cutting the interview short. As soon as you feel you have heard enough of an applicant's biased or stereotyped comments, you should write down what the applicant said, thank him or her for coming in, and then stand up and extend your hand.

Your applicant's comments are inappropriate in any workplace, and the fact that he voiced them in a job interview shows that he is totally clueless. There are many outstanding applicants in today's labor pool, and you don't need to hire any from the shallow end.

Gift of gab or blab

Q. I just interviewed an applicant for a sales position, and I was not impressed. He talked almost the whole time and never knew when to stop. A few other people here also interviewed him, and they want to hire him. They say he has the gift of gab and that's exactly what is needed in a good salesperson. I don't think they are correct. Do you?

A. Many successful salespeople are, in fact, good talkers, but the most successful salespeople have something more powerful than the gift of gab. They have the gift of listening, and that is what separates them from the rest of the pack.

Truly effective salespeople spend a great deal of time trying to understand their customers. In fact, some studies show that at least 80 percent of their time in a sales presentation is spent listening. In many cases, salespeople with the so-called gift of gab are the ones who keep pushing a product on a customer, regardless of what the customer needs. They often do very little to understand the customer's needs, build trust, and build a successful working relationship. This is hardly professional selling.

Nonetheless, it is entirely possible that your sales applicant is very good at what he does, and perhaps his style fits perfectly with your company's style and objectives. In addition, if you really want to know more about him, you should get his permission to talk with some of his references. He may have the gift of gab, but his references will tell you if that gift is worth anything.

The rush job

Q. During a recent job interview, the interviewer seemed to be rushing me. He cut me off on some answers, and I don't feel I got my best information out. What's the best thing to do when rushed in a job interview?

A. When you feel you are being stampeded through an interview, the first question to ask is whether you actually need a shove. One of the most important steps in a job interview is to keep your answers brief, clear, and to the point.

Assuming you did not turn each answer into an acceptance speech, the real question focuses on the interviewer's behavior. The problem is that there can be countless reasons for rushing you. For example, perhaps this was a brief preliminary interview, or maybe the interviewer had a last-minute appointment or was just plain inept.

The next time you feel that an interviewer is in fast-forward, you can politely yet assertively mention that there are some key points you would like to add, and then briefly state them. In a job interview, you are a salesperson selling your labor. Do you think a good salesperson would hold back the best information about his or her product?

A powerful persuasive strategy is to match your behavior with the person whom you are trying to influence. The next time you encounter a job interviewer who is in a big hurry, pick up the pace in your answers, as this can increase the likelihood of the interviewer picking you.

Shine it on

Q. I just interviewed an applicant for a sales position and I noticed that his shoes were very scuffed. If this is how he takes care of his appearance when trying to get a job, I figure he'll do the same thing when he tries to sell our products. Should I pass on him?

A. Just because an applicant's shoes are not polished does not mean that his sales skills are not polished. There are plenty of great salespeople whose shoes have scuff marks on the scuff marks, but if you focus on an applicant's feet in the interview process, you may be overlooking some vastly more important feats.

Obviously, if this individual is going to be selling shoe polish or other related products, then you would have a right to question his judgment. However, beyond that, there are far more significant factors to consider.

For example, you will get better predictive data by focusing on this applicant's work history. Do his experiences indicate that he has the knowledge, skills, abilities, persistence, and motivation to sell for your company?

You can give him work sample questions and simulations to further check out his sales skills. If he sails through the interview and his references verify his excellence, then there is no need for you to give him the boot.

Applicant bashing

Q. I was interviewed for a job and a week later I got a phone call from the person who interviewed me. She said I was rejected, and then she made some insulting comments about the way I handled the interview. I am disappointed about being rejected, and I am angry over the negative feedback. Should I call her back or let it go?

A. It's normal to feel dejected after being rejected, but it's abnormal for any interviewer to add insults to this injury. This kind of treatment does give some you additional insight into the company.

Your feelings of disappointment and distress are most likely going to dissipate over time, especially if you line up some other interviews or even land a job. If you have no other irons in the fire at this point, you are likely to keep fuming over this shabby treatment.

Either way, if you find that you cannot shake the negative feelings, you should give this interviewer a call. Let her know how you feel, and then ask her to clarify what she was saying. She might apologize for going so far off base, or perhaps she will provide you with a piece of data that could help you in a future interview or job.

Just as some retailers use professional shoppers to see how their salespeople are treating customers, perhaps it would make sense for employers to use professional applicants to see how their interviewers are treating or mistreating job-seekers.

Actively pursuing mediocrity

Q. We are a family business, and one of the managers who works for us hires weak employees. He has the highest turnover in the company, and we have told him to raise the bar, but he continues to bring on employees with skill levels beneath what we need. How do we take care of this?

A. When a manager hires weak employees, it can be a sign that he or she is a weak employee, too.

On the one hand, it is possible that this manager hires lesser qualified individuals because he is not adequately trained in the screening process and does not know the techniques to separate outstanding from outrageous candidates. If this is the case, he should be provided with more training, and this can include spending time with him during the hiring process.

On the other hand, it is possible that this manager is a little wobbly when it comes to personal security, and he feels threatened by having strong employees under him. This type of manager operates under the mistaken assumption that he is safe in his job if no one under him is qualified for it. He needs to understand that high turnover and questionable departmental performance and productivity place everyone in the department on the watch list.

It is also important for him to understand that managers who hire stronger employees not only have departments that operate better, but also make themselves more promotable.

At the same time, let him know that if he refuses to raise the bar, management may bar his raise, or even worse.

Input not included

Q. I am a department manager and one of the senior managers asked three of us to jointly interview with an applicant for an important financial position. After the interview, the three of us discussed the applicant carefully and agreed that he did not have the right experience. We told the senior manager, and he went ahead and hired him without any further discussion with us. We are annoyed and wonder if we should say something to the senior manager.

A. It's normal to be annoyed when you expend time on a project, only to find that your input is put aside. Your senior manager certainly has the final say-so in hiring, but because he asked you to help in the screening process, he should have discussed his thinking with you prior to making the job offer.

It is a good idea for you to let your manager know how you feel. The discussion should not focus on the lack of qualifications of the applicant, because he is an applicant no more. Rather, your objective should be to discuss the process.

Let your manager know that you appreciate being part of the decision, and you believe it would be even more helpful and productive if there were an opportunity to discuss your findings before he places an offer on the table. If he agrees, then the matter is resolved, at least for the future. If he gets difficult, perhaps your work schedule will be too busy for you to interview anyone else for him next time.

Who are we?

Q. I just interviewed a well-qualified applicant who answered most of his questions with the word *we*. I had a hard time figuring out what he individually accomplished. I even mentioned this to him, but he did not change his style. How does this applicant sound to you?

A. Interviewers are hearing the word *we,* more often these days because applicants are being advised to avoid the word *I.* The idea is that an applicant will sound more like a team player if he or she sticks with "we."

Interviewers do indeed tire of hearing an applicant who met every single objective solely on his or her own without ever mentioning the support provided by some of the significant others on the job. In many cases, it is more than appropriate to mention the contributions of others in meeting one's goals.

However, when applicants overplay the team aspect, they actually raise two red flags. Firstly, by emphasizing teamwork so heavily, the applicant may actually be masking a teamwork problem. Secondly, when an applicant ignores feedback from an interviewer, there can be real questions about his or her insight into the feelings of others, along with questions about his or her listening skills.

At the very least, "we" should move very slowly with this applicant.

Chapter 2

New Employee on the Block

When new employees arrive on the scene, many seize the moment as an unparalleled opportunity to demonstrate their finely-tuned abilities to act as consummate jerks. At the same time, this moment is an equally perfect opportunity for their new associates to demonstrate that they will not be outdone as jerks. In either case, when there are new employees, there are new antics that clearly fall under the heading of jerky behaviors.

In some cases, the bizarre behaviors of new hires or existing employees do not instantly appear. In fact, initially, new working relationships can be quite amicable and comfortable. However, given time—in some cases a very short period of time—the latent jerk tendencies of some new employees or the staff around them can jump into high gear.

Having new leadership is a major change in the lives of the employees, and they typically approach a new leader with a combination of concern, trepidation, and anxiety. If that new leader quickly demonstrates behaviors that point to respect and trust for the employees, some of the employees' reticence can be reduced, and some of the barriers on the road to a productive working relationship can be knocked down. However, for those new leaders intent on acting like jerks, the road will be very bumpy indeed.

Demonstrating to their new world that they are jerks is not a quality that is reserved only for senior level employees. While there is no question that some newly-hired managers can create inordinate problems for their subordinates through such inane actions as transforming into harsh and dictatorial leaders, or even invisible leaders, there are new rank and file employees who can demonstrate equally outlandish behaviors, such as filling a new office with stuffed animals.

This situation can be compounded by the jerk behaviors of existing employees who await the arrival of the newest members of their team. Some of their more common behaviors include a combination of rejection, criticism, and ostracism. The existing employees wait for the new arrivals to fall into one of their traps, and then they pounce, hoping that their prey will head for the nearest exit.

In a new job, there can be scurrilous jerks lurking around every cubicle. And if the company is short on jerks, perhaps the new employee is destined to increase the jerk population.

And don't forget the worst combination of all: the new employee is a card-carrying jerk, and he or she comes face-to-face with coworkers who are carrying the same card.

Fortunately, there are proven steps in dealing with proven jerks in all of these quirky, jerky scenarios.

Transferring troubles

Q. I just received word that a problem employee is going to be transferred into my department. I have a very nice group of people here, and I am concerned about the impact this individual is going to have. What steps can you suggest to help make this transition smooth?

A. When a so-called "problem employee" is about to be transferred into another department, the real problem is the expectation that this individual is going to be a bundle of difficulties. If you expect to have trouble with this individual, you immediately increase the likelihood of finding it.

When managers have negative expectations about employees, they tend to act in a way that actually generates undesirable behaviors. At the same time, when managers expect positive behaviors from employees, they tend to act in a way that brings such behaviors out.

At this point, the best step is to approach this new employee with an open mind and positive expectations. After all, it is possible that this individual earned the label of problem employee because of his dealings with a coworker or boss who may actually have caused the questionable behavior in the first place.

And if it turns out that this individual has a scorched reputation for a reason, you should apply the same standards and counseling that would be used for any of your employees. Depending upon his response, you should have no problem figuring out what your next step should be.

Rush to prejudgment

Q. One of my friends worked under the new manager who is being transferred to our department. When I asked my friend to tell me about her, he said she is temperamental, touchy, and impossible to please. Do you have any tips on how to deal with this type of person?

A. The best tip is to wait until the transfer is complete and she actually starts managing your department. All you have right now is a batch of labels from your friend, and although he may have had his share of problems working with her, it is possible that he was the problem.

It is interesting to note that the terms he uses to describe her sound like sex-role stereotypes. Words such as *temperamental* and *touchy* are often used by males to describe female managers with whom they have difficulties. While his description may be accurate, it may also be a reflection of deeper issues going on in his head.

An additional tip is to clear your own head of the negative expectations regarding this manager. If you expect difficulties in your working relationship with her, you are far more likely to encounter them. When people expect problems with others, they typically act in a way that draws them out.

Meet your new manager with an open mind and try to let excellence permeate your performance. From that point, you should let the chips fall where they may, but don't start things off with one on your shoulder.

Before and after

Q. When my current boss interviewed me for this job, he was friendly, funny, and easygoing. Now that I work here, he is mean and completely different from the way he was in the interview. I wonder why he would do this and if there is anything I can do about it.

A. The reason your boss acted like a human being during the interview is that if he acted like himself, neither you nor any other reasonable applicant would have accepted the job. He is obviously a pretty good actor, although he has trouble staying in character during the second act.

When dealing with a manager who adheres to the Jekyll and Hyde theory of management, there are a few steps to consider. First, the next time he is mean to you, let him see how his behavior is working against his own objectives. He needs to understand that by being mean to you, not only is he generating stress and dissatisfaction, he is also undercutting performance and productivity.

One of the most powerful words in the persuasive process is "guarantee." Tell him that you guarantee that if he can treat you more professionally, your productivity will improve. Be sure to give him a clear idea of what you mean by professional treatment.

In the long run, the best way to avoid this type of problem is to screen your future boss as carefully as he or she would screen you. Sometimes a few words with your future coworkers can tell you whether the boss knows how to act like a manager or merely knows how to act.

Where is Human Resources?

Q. I am a manager in a company that has approximately 200 employees. A new human resources director was hired two months ago, and I have yet to meet him. He has sent out some memos, but he has never held a meeting with the employees, nor has he set foot in our department that has 10 employees. Should I contact him?

A. It sounds as though your company has a human resources director whose skills in the area of humans and resources may be a little thin.

Even if he walked into an absolutely overwhelming personnel disaster, he has overlooked a key opportunity to build credibility, trust, and communication with the rest of the employees.

One of the more enduring criticisms of traditional personnel managers is that they tend to generate too much paperwork and too many memos. The fact that your new human resources director played the memo card is not the most promising start.

Although you do not want to sound as if you are telling him how to do his job, you can call him, introduce yourself, and invite him to one of your meetings so that he can meet your staff. The actions that he takes in response to this call will tell you a great deal about his style as a human resources professional. Hopefully, he will come to the meeting prepared not only to discuss the key human resources programs, issues, and objectives, but also prepared to listen. At the same time, if his response to your overture is another memo or two, stand back because masses of paperwork are just around the corner.

The resistance movement

Q. I joined this company as a manager about six months ago. There is a core of employees that has been resistant to me and difficult to manage from day one. They have been with the company for a long time, and they definitely have an attitude. What is the best way to deal with them?

A. If these long-term employees have any interest in becoming even longer-term employees, they need to understand the necessity of working with you, not against you. For the past six months, it sounds as though you have been rather tolerant in your dealings with them, and this has generated a rather intolerable situation in return.

The best way to approach this situation is by having frequent contact and two-way communication with this group, and by trying to include their inputs in establishing plans and goals for the department. In addition, these employees should be encouraged to develop their own performance goals that can contribute to those of the department. Let them see that you are willing to provide active guidance and support throughout the process.

There is a related step that is also worth considering. Within this kind of employee grouping, there is typically a leader who plays a major role in determining acceptable behaviors and attitudes. While it may be difficult for you to sell your ideas to the group, it is relatively easy for this person to do so. You probably already know who this leader is, and the next step is to meet with him or her. Let this person understand your respect for the experience and expertise of the long-term employees, and then set some clear expectations regarding the kind of leadership role that you would want this person to play among the group. This person should understand the advantages and opportunities associated with playing such a role.

If the employees do not respond to your positive and supportive approach, then it is appropriate for you to implement your back-up style. In a word, the employees should understand that there is a term that describes their resistant behavior perfectly: insubordination. Let them know the specific sanctions that will be applied when their behavior contradicts the established rules, standards, and performance expectations.

Long term employees are an asset to the organization, but if they have an attitude that places them above it, they can easily become a liability.

Not the job I accepted

Q. I was hired here approximately three months ago, and the job is completely different from the way it was described. There was supposed to be lots of people contact, and that's minimal. There was not supposed to be much administrative work or paperwork, and now it seems that's all I do. What do you suggest I do?

A. There is always a difference between a job and a job description, but it should not be so great that any similarity between the two is purely coincidental. Many companies today are reconfiguring jobs because of economic constraints and cutbacks, and many people are picking up responsibilities that used to be part of phased-out positions. However, that still does not mean you should be hired for one job and placed in another.

The best step for you to take is to discuss the situation with your manager. However, if you come in and complain about having too much paperwork, that is not going to win many points.

It will make more sense to approach him or her with questions. For example, ask your manager about the plans for your position. You can specifically ask if there are plans to include more people contact in the position, because this was a key part of the original design and is also a key area where you are able to add value.

Listen carefully to what your manager says, because his plans are going to have a real impact on yours.

Rapid hire...rapid fire

Q. Three of us interviewed a candidate for a department manager position, and we all thought she was terrific. We quickly hired her, and now we find that she is completely different. She is dictatorial and over-controlling, and she interrupts everyone. What do we do now?

A. Sometimes an applicant can appear to be a real beauty, only to turn into a beast once he or she is on the job. During the employment process, applicants are in a sales mode and try to be as likable, charming, and endearing as is humanly possible.

When you say you quickly hired her, that's often a euphemism for hiring someone without taking reference checks. If that's what happened here, you are definitely forewarned for the next personable applicant.

In the meantime, the best step is to give this individual some specific performance-based feedback. Do not use labels such as "dictatorial" or "over-controlling." Rather, talk to her about situations when she showed these kinds of behaviors, and then give her some suggestions and even examples of more productive ways to act.

The next step will depend on her reaction. If she truly listens to your feedback and tries to make some adjustments, give her positive feedback whenever you see the changed behavior. However, if she comes back with interruptions and defensiveness, then she needs to understand the consequences associated with these types of behaviors.

There are very good reasons for companies to have probationary periods, and she is one of those reasons.

Is everybody happy?

Q. I am a manager, and I was just transferred to another branch to replace a manager who was terminated. He was very lenient, and I'm not. I'm already hearing that the employees are not as happy as they used to be. What do you suggest?

A. When it comes to managers, "lenient" is often a code word for inept. These are the managers who want to be loved by their employees, and they figure that the best way to accomplish this is to let the employees do whatever they want. The department keeps on running, but no one knows if it's coming or going.

When top management spots the problem, one thing that typically ends up going is the manager, while one thing that typically ends up coming is a replacement. If the branch was a nine-to-five happy hour before you arrived, it is only natural that the troops are not as happy now, regardless of your managerial style.

At the same time, it is important for you to do a quick management-style check. If you have entered the branch with answers to everything, to the level that you even have answers for which there are no conceivable questions, you will encounter tremendous resistance regardless of your predecessor's style. In addition to resistance, you will find a mixture of dissatisfaction, disappointment, and, of course, unhappiness.

Your best approach is to make sure that you have a good deal of two-way communication with the employees. If there are some "quick-fix" problems that you can correct, do so. Let them see that you are a communicative and responsive leader who listens to what they have to say.

As for their happiness, your objective as a manager is not specifically to make the employees happy. At the same time, you can do so without having to turn your branch into an amusement park.

Try to get to know the employees as individuals, and work with them to formulate goals that will meet their needs as well as those of the branch. With appropriate coaching and recognition, you can help your employees be more productive and meet these goals. When this happens, the direct outcome is that they will sense higher levels of achievement, competence, and personal effectiveness. The indirect outcome is that they will also feel happier. And, so will you.

Out of alignment

Q. We promoted a loyal employee into management, but he seems to align himself with his subordinates rather than with the company on every issue that arises. How do we get him to act more like a manager?

A. While loyalty is an important factor to consider when promoting employees into management, it is equally important to note that pets are loyal but that does not qualify them for management. Part of the problem may be that you placed too much emphasis on loyalty and too little on the real factors that predict managerial success.

If you really want to know if an employee has a decent chance of succeeding in management, look also to see if he or she is already showing any behaviors that are found in successful managers. For example, is this person playing a leadership role in the department? Is the person particularly effective in organizing his or her work and perhaps that of others? Can you rely on this person for clear and accurate communication, whether written or oral?

If your new manager still identifies with his old pals, the next step is to review the amount of guidance, support, and training that he is receiving from you and your management team. It is possible that he is floundering because your company's approach is to toss new managers into the corporate waters and let them sink or swim on their own. If this is the case, he simply swam back to his friends.

It may also be helpful for you to give him a clearer idea of the kinds of behaviors that you expect him to display as a manager. He will need feedback on any of his actions that undercut his managerial effectiveness, as well as specific guidance on how to handle such situations in the future.

If there are key issues about which he feels the employees are right and management is wrong, advise him that he is part of the management team and should be discussing such concerns with his fellow managers. He will need to see that your leadership team is receptive and responsive to his ideas and suggestions, and is oriented toward taking swift action when appropriate.

Your objective is to provide him with all of the resources he needs to succeed in management. If he still cannot act like a manager, perhaps there is an understudy who can.

Blasts from the past

Q. I am relatively new on the job, and most of the people I work with have been here for quite a while. The problem is that they constantly refer to stories and experiences from the past, and I am left out of the conversation. I am tired of this, but I don't know what to do about it.

A. What you are seeing is typical clique behavior, but it obviously does not click with you. Part of the problem is that every organization has its history, humor, culture, and even a climate. Some are warm and hospitable, while others can be nothing short of an ice age. It sounds as if your company is parked somewhere on the cooler end of the scale.

You are also experiencing the new-kid-on-the-block syndrome. At first, everyone can seem distant and unfriendly, but this can change in time, particularly as you get to know the kids individually, rather than in a pack. One approach is for you to try to take some extra time to get to know your fellow employees on a more individualized basis. There will be some who can talk about issues relevant to the twenty-first century, and who will also be interested in what you have to say.

It is important to remember that there are always leaders in these groups who set the style and standards for the others to follow. If the leader is open, receptive, and responsive to you, the others will, more than likely, follow suit. This means that it will be helpful for you to try to identify the leader and get to know him or her on a more individualized basis, so that the next time the group starts to reminisce for the umpteenth time about some inane event, the leader may put on the brakes and try to include you in the conversation.

In the meantime, it may be worthwhile for you to seek out other newer employees and open the communication lines with them. After all, you already have a good deal in common with them.

On a longer term basis, it will be important for you to remember how you are feeling today, particularly when you ultimately become a longer-term employee and deal with newly-hired personnel.

While a company's climate is about as easy to change as the weather, you and some of the other newer employees can start the process of corporate warming.

Totally stuffed

Q. We just hired a new person for telephone sales, and she brought in a huge number of stuffed animals and put them all over her work area. I don't approve of how it looks, and I am concerned that they will prevent her from finding important paperwork and files on her desk. What is the best way to get her to take some of these things home?

A. Because you have no evidence that her fluffy menagerie is interfering with her work or the work of others, it's probably too early to ask her to disband the flock. However, if the herd is already interfering with her orientation, getting in the way of others, or creating a safety problem, you should discuss the matter with her.

In such as case, the best step is to give her the specifics about the problems that her pack is causing. You should not insult her or her furry pals.

At the same time, you may be overreacting to her collection. If there is no true work-related problem associated with the pack, then your best step is to let some time pass and then look at her sales numbers and her ability to access needed information.

If her pets are preventing her from reaching her potential and becoming a productive member of your team, she should be advised of the specific problems. It's a good thing for employees to make their offices comfortable and homey, but not when it's too much of a good thing.

Upward mobility and hostility

Q. I am the newest employee in my department, and I believe I have been doing excellent work. When a supervisory position opened up, I was very fortunate and the position was given to me. Now there is serious resentment toward me from several employees who have been here longer. How do I deal with it?

A. When a new employee is promoted over others who have been around longer, that often promotes a good deal of resentment as well. Unfortunately, there is no quick fix.

The other employees are most likely feeling a combination of jealousy, frustration, and inequitable treatment, no matter how much you may have deserved the promotion. The only way for this negativity to simmer down is for you to demonstrate that management clearly made a great choice. This means that your leadership style should be communicative, ethical, respectful, responsive, and focused on the needs and motivations of the individuals whom you supervise.

One simple step that can help you start out on the right foot is to correct a nagging problem in the department, such as by getting a broken copier fixed or getting another sorely needed computer. The idea is to let the employees literally see that there are going to be some real improvements with you as supervisor. Beyond that, you should take some classes in supervising. This will not only help you become the supervisor that management envisioned, but will also help you become the manager that you envisioned.

On time or else

Q. Our new manager is very strict, and he said that prompt attendance at his staff meetings is essential. Then he added that if we are late, he will lock the door. We thought he was kidding, but when I arrived a few minutes late because I was on a business phone call, I was locked out. The only message from the manager was for me to get to the next meeting on time. How does this sound to you?

A. When managers resort to locked doors, it is often a symptom of a locked mind. After all, this kind of thinking has locked out such concepts as treating employees with respect and trust, managing with some flexibility, and focusing on the employee's individual needs and responsibilities.

There is no question that employees should attend meetings on time, and that expectation should be clearly voiced to all of them. However, there can be any number of important work-related circumstances that can cause an employee to be late. Threatening to lock an employee out of a meeting implies that a manager does not mind if that employee hangs up on a customer, ignores a key question from a coworker, or walks out in the middle of an important discussion with an associate.

And further, when employees miss an entire meeting, as opposed to missing a few minutes, someone is going to have to take even more time to update them. If your manager wants employees to act as adults, he needs to treat them as adults. Locking employees out of a meeting creates an adversarial relationship, and that can only lead to an adverse outcome.

Doubting promises

Q. During a job interview, I was promised all sorts of things that have never materialized. I have continued to ask for them after I accepted the job, but management just ignores my requests. Do you have ideas about why companies lie and what I should do?

A. In this unpromising situation, the company probably wanted you on board very badly and was willing to say anything to get you to commit. The hope was that once you were on payroll, you would see the company's other wonderful qualities and would think less about broken promises. Of course, the more common reaction is to think less of the company itself.

Companies that engage in deceitful hiring practices run all sorts of risks, such as increased levels of dissatisfaction, distraction, and turnover, and even legal exposure. When companies use an underhanded hiring strategy, employees often respond with their own exit strategy.

At this point, you have nothing to lose by continuing to approach management regarding the unfilled promises. However, rather than repeatedly asking, you may find more success by using more of a sales approach. Let management see the many benefits that will come to them if they keep the commitments. Be sure to phrase such benefits in language that meets their needs, such as in terms of profit, growth, success, and achievement.

If management continues down this road, then perhaps you need to seek a more promising work situation.

Chapter 3

Bothered by Bullying Bosses

This is the era of the bully at work, and in any anthology of jerks, bullies have merited their own special place. More thank five years ago, there were certainly bullies, but they were not a prevalent force in the workplace. Bullies would appear here and there, but they did not overpopulate the corporate landscape and they were not adored or idolized. In fact, the whole issue of bullies at work was on such a back burner that the word, "bully," did not even appear in the index of the 1999 edition of this book or in most other management books at the time.

What a difference a half a decade makes. These days it is difficult to pick up a newspaper or turn on the television without finding some kind of feature that focuses on bullies at work. Employees in companies across America are encountering more and more of these managerial monsters, and the reactions are varied indeed.

In some companies, bullies are regarded as tough leaders who build strong employees and even stronger productivity. Unfortunately, anything you might read that fosters this point of view belongs in the fiction section.

Bullies are abusive, abrasive, threatening, and self-serving individuals who continuously pound their employees into submission. The lucky employees are those who escape, although the damage wreaked upon them can last for a career.

Many consultants and educators still advise people who work for bullies to weather the storm and try to deal with them during the few calm periods between their storms. This can be an effective approach, but now there are other approaches that can work even better, especially those that focus upon acting assertively right back at the bully.

Because many bullies act as though they are two-year-olds, it is interesting and ironic to note that some of the newest research that provides insight into the best ways to deal with bullies has come from studies in pediatrics, and not from management researchers. When two-year-olds dig their heels in and throw a tantrum, pediatric research shows that one of the best ways for parents to deal with them is to dig their own heels in and mirror some of the behaviors right back at the toddlers. In the workplace, there are times when employees can deal more effectively with their oversized toddlers by using similar techniques.

Many people are suffering from the destructive antics of bullies at work in many different ways. Fortunately, there are many different ways to counteract these bullies.

Refuse the abuse

Q. My manager is overly critical of just about everything I do. In my last review, some of his remarks were very hurtful, even though my work was definitely satisfactory. He said I need to understand that he is "brutally honest." How do you deal with someone such as this?

A. To be honest, people who claim they are "brutally honest" are often rather abusive. Such people think that the phrase, "brutally honest," gives them license to tear into someone else. This behavior is actually another form of bullying, and it does not belong in the workplace or any other place.

People who act like this are not likely to change, and that limits your options. If you are in a job where you do not have much contact with him, and the job offers many other satisfying elements, you may be able to hold your nose and report to him.

However, if his twisted honesty is taking a toll on you, then you need to address it. By allowing yourself to be subjected to his unkind comments, you are only going to hear more of them. The next time he launches into you, dig in your own heels and tell him that his approach is upsetting you and interfering with your work, and you want it to stop, now.

If it continues, you should speak with his manager. Once you do so, it should not take long for you to figure out your next step. It may be out the door, and that just might be a step in the right direction.

Brow-beaten by the bully

Q. My manager gave me a brief assignment and I completed it on time and correctly, but he tore into me and criticized the work up and down. I showed him, in black and white, that he was wrong, and then he said he did not care. He has not talked to me since and it's been a few days. What do I do now?

A. It does not sound as though your manager can actually manage. In the first place, this business of tearing into an employee is terrible. In most cases, when managers engage in this juvenile behavior, they are displaying immaturity, lack of self-control, and probably a dose of self-doubt. The fact that he said he did not care after being proven wrong furthers the point.

The best step to take depends upon what you know about this person's track record. Managers who treat others this way have typically done so numerous times in the past. Such an outburst is rarely an isolated event. As a result, take a look at this person's past performance. If you're new to the company, ask around and you will hear about his typical response pattern.

Some of these managers crawl back to the targeted employees and apologize, while some act as if nothing ever happened, and still others wait for the employees to approach them. There is probably a well-worn path at your company, and all you need to do is find it.

You might want to step back from the incident and see if there is a bigger message here. For example, if this type of managerial behavior is acceptable in the company, is this company acceptable to you?

Mean and meaner

Q. Our manager makes all sorts of mean comments to us. Whenever we voice any complaints or suggestions, his response is that if we don't enjoy working here, there are 10 people who will gladly take our job. That is the end of the discussion. How do we deal with someone such as this?

A. In the first place, his numbers our wrong. There is no way that 10 people are willing to take your job if they knew about him.

He may have the title of manager, but he is not acting as if he is one. A manager who makes mean-spirited comments to his employees generates dissatisfaction and distrust, and typically shows marginal managerial skills in other areas as well. It is possible that senior management is already aware that he is a weak link, and that he is managing like the missing link.

Because your manager has demonstrated his skill in silencing discussions before they get started, several of you should approach the next level of management to discuss your concerns. One of the most effective ways to structure this meeting is to present specific examples of your manager's questionable actions, and then ask the senior manager what he or she suggests you do from this point.

It is possible that this manager will commit to look into the situation and get back to you within a specified period of time. It is also possible that you will be ignored or even chastised. This manager's reaction will tell you a great deal about where the company is going and whether you should be going elsewhere.

Tease? Oh, please!

Q. My manager makes remarks that can be hurtful and degrading, and when I call him on it, he always says that he is just teasing. He says that he doesn't mean any harm and it is all done in fun. What can I do?

A. When it comes to managing, your manager is out to lunch, out to breakfast, and dinner, as well. He can claim that his words are all in fun and mean no harm, but his intent is irrelevant. The impact on you is hurtful, and that is all that matters.

His behaviors fall directly under the category of bullying, and such antics are totally out of place in today's work environment. In fact, they are out of touch in any of today's environments, whether at work, school, or home.

Although you have called him on these behaviors, he really needs more of a wake-up call. The next time he hurls one of these comments at you, tell him in a firm and businesslike way that this is just the type comment that you have discussed with him in the past. Let him know that his words are very upsetting and distressing to you, and this type of behavior has to stop now. Then add that you hope you will not have to take any further action to deal with it.

If he has even a shred of insight, decency, or reality, he will get the message. If he overlooks the message, you should look over him and speak with someone at the next level of management.

Take a stand, not a seat

Q. I am a legal secretary, and my boss is often moody, rude, abrupt, impatient, and unfriendly, and gets very defensive if I even hint about any of this. He said he does not have to apologize to me because I am not his wife. I am doing a good job, and it is hard to find another job. Any advice?

A. You are dealing with a boss who has more baggage than a 747 on a holiday weekend. His comment about his wife does not belong in any business discussion, and he has no right to be taking out any of his personal frustrations on you.

He is a classic bully, and his behavior is only going to get worse unless you intervene. You should tell him on the spot that his behavior is unacceptable and inappropriate, and you are not going to stand for it any more. Research is now showing that it can also help if you try to mirror some of his physical behaviors and speech patterns.

At the same time, because he flips in and out of his bully mode, you can also try the old-fashioned approach where you can discuss the situation with him between storms. Show him how his behaviors have led to errors and delays, and then let him see how much better you and the department can operate if he will cooperate.

He does not hold all of the cards. You can go to his boss if he has one. In addition, you are a skilled, knowledgeable, and trained employee. No matter what your boss says, he does not want to go through the time, cost, and likely turnover associated with an attempt to replace you. Granted that you do not want to change jobs, do not forget that even in a questionable economy, there are still excellent opportunities for excellent employees.

It's a scream

Q. I am an administrative assistant, and my boss was starting a meeting and he asked me to go down the hall and tell another manager who was supposed to attend that the meeting was about to begin. I stuck my head in the manager's office and he yelled at me and said he knows the meeting is starting and he'll be there when he can. I left and simply told my manager what he said. Should I tell my manager about the screaming?

A. A work environment should be a yell-free zone. You were simply doing your job, and it sounds as though you carried out this task correctly, but still found yourself targeted by this screamer.

People who yell at work typically have more baggage than most conveyor belts at O'Hare Airport. They are walking around with a large dose of emotional immaturity, and yelling is their way of flexing power and dominating others.

You should tell your manager about what happened. Don't do any labeling, such as by calling this manager a baby. Rather, just tell your manager that you are concerned about this manager's reaction to your request, and then specifically describe what happened. Don't be surprised if your manager directly or indirectly indicates that this is not the first time the manager in question has acted questionably.

As for the future, hopefully your manager will speak to him about this outburst, because these antics present a broad array of potential problems and exposure for the company. In the meantime, the best steps you can take are in the opposite direction of the screamer.

Bully for you

Q. I was at a meeting with several other managers today and the senior manager running the meeting attacked one of the others because of a very minor mistake. As the meeting was closing, I mentioned a point that needed further discussion, and he jumped at me and told me I was wrong and declared the meeting over. How do you deal with someone such as this?

A. Words such as "attacked" and "jumped" are not exactly high on the list of behaviors from today's best managers. In fact, these behaviors are the exact opposite of what you would find in truly excellent companies.

In excellent companies, people obviously still make mistakes, but they are not torn apart or insulted for doing so. Mistakes are discussed and reviewed, but this is done as a building process, not a demolition project. When employees sense they will be thrashed for an error, they become far less creative, daring, imaginative, and productive.

You are in the best position to know what to do with your bully. If he runs hot-and-cold, there may be a time when you can approach him and talk about what happened here, and even give him some insight into the impact of his behavior. However, if he is a

24/7 bully, you should try to keep your contact with him to a minimum and consider speaking with his manager.

The larger question is whether your company tolerates and even condones his behavior. If his behavior is standard for your organization, the question is whether you should be working somewhere else with higher standards.

Being tough versus being rough

Q. There has been much written in the papers and online recently about a nominee for an important government position who uses a tough managerial style. I think that being tough is an integral part of being an effective leader. I do not believe that being tough should ever stop someone from holding a top leadership position; on the contrary, I think it should be a requirement. What do you think?

A. There are times when effective leaders do need to be tough, but there is a difference between toughness and bullying. Today's most effective managers are able to vary their leadership style depending upon the individuals involved and various situational factors.

There can be times when such leaders are indeed tough, decisive, and firm, such as when time constraints are limited and the potential outcomes are critical. At the same time, such leaders can use a more communicative and participative style in other situations, such as when the pressure or stakes are not as great.

However, there is never an appropriate time for a manager to bully his or her employees. When managers threaten, harass, degrade, or intimidate their employees, they are not managing at all. A manager who throws things at his or her employees or chases them up and down the halls is not showing that he or she is firm or tough, but is actually showing weakness. They are weak when it comes to understanding management per se, as well as understanding the people whom they supervise.

Truly effective managers focus on their employees as individuals and strive to treat them with respect and trust, regardless of the situation.

Managers who stray from this approach soon find that their best employees stray from them.

Insensitive and in trouble

Q. Over the past year and a half, I have worked for the same manager. During this period, I have put on some weight, and recently he has made some insulting comments about it. I have told him that I don't appreciate it, but he still does it. I'm not looking for trouble or lawsuits. I just want him to stop. What do you suggest?

A. You are working for an insecure and insensitive individual who thinks that part of managing is bullying. Obviously, he is wrong in every sense of the word.

You have been rather kind in your comments to him, and he may sense that your mild words are a sign of weakness. Telling him that you do not appreciate the insults is actually telling him what he wants to hear, namely that his bullying is upsetting you. He needs to be dealt with more forcefully.

The next time he makes an insulting comment, address it on the spot and tell him that you do not approve of his remarks, they are hurting you and interfering with your ability to do your work, and you want them to stop right now so that you will not have to take any additional action on this matter.

If he does not understand this verbal two-by-four, you should approach his manager. Growing numbers of companies are taking swift corrective action in these types of situations, as there are compelling humanistic and monetary reasons for doing so.

Decibel management

Q. My question is about an organizational behavior that is creating a lot of stress, mostly at work. I consider raising my voice different from yelling. In your opinion, is there a difference? What can I do to have others understand the difference?

A. There may well be a difference between vein-popping yelling and a raised voice, but neither should be ringing through the halls of the workplace. It sounds as though you are saying that yelling at others in the workplace is not acceptable, but raising your voice is. The truth of the matter is that neither is acceptable, as they are both forms of bullying and intimidation.

The reason that many people do not differentiate between raising your voice and yelling is the result of perception. You might regard your loud words as a raised voice, while those whom you are addressing can view your heightened vocalizing as yelling. In order to stop the problem, simply stop raising your voice.

Effective management today is premised on treating employees with respect and trust. If you have an employee who is performing poorly, engaging in questionable behavior, or failing in any other way, he or she certainly needs to hear from you. However, raising your voice is not the way to get your message across. In fact, when you raise your voice, regardless of the decibel level, most recipients are going to block out whatever you are saying.

If you really want to be heard, speak softer. People will actually have to pay more attention to hear your quiet voice. Raising your voice is only going to raise the hackles of your employees, and perhaps raise the eyebrows of your managers.

Rants by the tyrant

Q. Our manager is a tyrant. She yells and screams at most of us, makes unreasonable demands, and generally treats us poorly. The turnover in our department is the highest in the company. We have gone to senior management and told them about this, but they do not seem to care. Is there anything else we should be doing?

A. Not with this manager. If you genuinely enjoy working for this company, then your next move should be to transfer out of this department as soon as possible. However, that still leaves the larger question of why you want to remain in this company at all. Top management has clearly demonstrated that they do not care about your ideas, inputs, and concerns, and they are obviously willing to keep a manager who treats employees with reckless disdain, and that's on a good day.

By failing to do anything about your manager, senior management would rather deal with a high degree of turnover than a high degree of employee concern. That makes very little sense, not only in humanistic terms, but in economic terms as well. The best companies today strive to treat their employees with respect and trust, but you seem to have found a company that prefers to treat them like dirt.

This is a very good time to step back and take a look at where you want your career to go. At various points in your work life, you will get subtle and not-so-subtle messages about your career direction. You are at one of those points, and management is giving you one of those messages.

The offensive lines

Q. Our manager has this habit of saying, "I know I shouldn't say this," before coming out with a disgusting or degrading comment. He gets a big laugh out of this, as do some of the followers around here, but many of us are offended. What do you do with a manager such as this?

A. If there is a course in remedial management, enroll him in it. This person is not a manager, but rather is a bully, a buffoon, and a brat. He is also a walking liability for the company.

The idea that the phrase, "I know I shouldn't be saying this," somehow magically shields him from any possible repercussions for what may come out next is sheer folly. This type of behavior has a negative impact on employee satisfaction, teamwork, commitment, and productivity.

You and some of your associates should approach him on a businesslike basis and let him know your feelings. Be sure that he understands the present and potential costs that are associated with his behavior, and clearly indicate that you would appreciate it stopping.

If his offensive comments continue, you and your group should approach senior management. It is important for senior management to know that this is going on in your department, and it is even more important for you to know what senior management does about it.

Selective bullying

Q. There are about 20 people in our department, but the manager is mean to me. She yells and screams at me if I make the slightest mistake, but rarely raises her voice to the others. I hate to say it, but she makes me cry. What can I do?

A. The individual that you describe as a manager is not a manager at all—she is a bully. This is a person who skulks around the corporate playground, looking for someone to verbally beat up. More importantly, bullies do not get into battles with people who may give them a match, but search for people whom they think they can dominate.

If you want this nonsense to stop, your first move is to try to act more assertively. Naturally, that is easier said than done, and you may need to consider some assertiveness training.

Rather than waiting for the next time she pushes you around, you should meet with her in the moments when she is acting more like a human. Spell out the specific behaviors that are upsetting you, let her know exactly how you feel, and then indicate that the behaviors in question must stop now. Wrap up the meeting by letting her know that if this type of abuse and harassment continues, your next step will be to go to senior management or explore your legal options.

If the bully remains bullheaded, it is time to take that next step.

Management by hypocrisy

Q. Over a recent holiday weekend, according to my manager, he supposedly called me and I missed several pages. I assured him that my pager is always on and I would never ignore a page. He cursed at me and called me a liar. Meanwhile, he is notorious for ignoring pages, voicemail, and company e-mail. He has lied and threatened us with termination, and I've been told that his behavior is typical for this company. What should I do?

A. Your manager curses at you, threatens you, lies to you, calls you a liar, ignores communication to him, all of which are typical for this company, and you wonder what to do? Perhaps it is more appropriate to wonder why you are putting up with this nonsense in the first place.

Your manager is in the shallow end when it comes to management skills. He sounds far more like a bully, harasser, and abuser—not exactly the criteria one seeks in a leader. You and your associates can try to discuss your concerns with him, but because he dodges pages, voicemail, and e-mail, you can expect him to dodge you as well.

Assuming that you get nowhere with him, your next stop should be with senior management. However, if your manager's behavior is truly typical for this company, you should not expect much of a reaction at this level either.

The real person to approach in this matter is yourself, and the real question is why you are staying with this company. Employees deserve to be treated with respect and trust, and if you accept anything short of that, you are shortchanging your career.

From the horse's mouth

Q. I am in management, and I admit that I scream at my employees when necessary. If I really lose it, I apologize later. My people understand me and work hard for me. Now, some new young vice president has told me to tone it down. I've had a productive department for years, and I don't see why I should change.

A. Bosses who lose it with employees typically end up losing productivity, respect, and ultimately the employees themselves. There is simply no excuse for yelling at the employees.

It is very nice that you apologize after you really jump on them, but you are leaving out the essence of what makes an apology valid: Given a similar situation down the road, you should not repeat the behavior. By screaming at your employees, apologizing, and then screaming again later, the apology is rather hollow.

Your people may indeed work hard for you, but there probably is a high degree of resentment and turmoil beneath the surface. At best, they are tolerating your style, rather than being motivated by it. Employees tend to be far more productive under an individual who is fair, respectful, trusting, and able to manage his department and his anger.

The good news is that the new vice president senses that you have some real strengths. He has sent you a message, and now the question is whether you have the strength to do anything about it.

Thrown off track

Q. My manager has a packet on our health insurance that is supposed to be given to all of us. When I asked for mine, he came by my desk later and literally threw it at me and then walked away. I don't want to make a big deal out of nothing, but what should I do about this?

A. There is no good reason to throw anything at an employee unless it is an occasional compliment. It would have been particularly ironic if an airborne health insurance packet had injured you.

It is possible that your manager was in a huge rush and as he ran by your desk, he wanted to drop off the packet but misfired. At the same time, it is also possible that he is upset with something or someone, including you, and this was his immature way of showing it.

Either way, the best time to deal with this type of behavior is when it occurs. You could use a direct approach and ask what that was all about, but that could be perceived as an attack. A non-threatening way to get at the issue is to ask your manager if something is wrong. That can open the discussion and also cause him to think about what he did.

If the incident continues to remain on your mind, you can still approach your manager and ask the same question. The way that he responds is likely to provide the answer to many questions about him.

The bully's pull

Q. There is a very senior person here who is mean, divisive, and uncaring. I can't imagine why he is still on board. He is not team-oriented, and he demands that everything be done his way. People who report to him think he is a dictator. Why would a company keep someone such as this?

A. Even if this character is as disruptive, dysfunctional, and disliked as you describe, there can be any number of reasons why he has not been directed to the corporate off-ramp.

For example, he might be contributing mightily to the bottom line. Perhaps, in spite of himself, he is playing a key role in the company's financial success, and the company is reluctant to touch him.

There can also be political reasons behind his tenure. He may be connected to a key customer or to other sources of power in the industry, community, or even the government. Without him, there could be a major disruption in the company's ability to continue successfully.

It is also possible that the company feels obligated to him because of his earlier successes or contributions. Perhaps he provided introductions to key customers that are still sources of great revenue.

On the sinister side, he may know something about the company that could create real problems if such knowledge saw the light of day. Or, maybe his strong ties to the company are actually family ties.

You should try to learn more about what is going on here. By understanding the company's reason for keeping him around, you can better decide if you want to stick around.

Chapter 4

Managers Who Still Don't Get It

As was the case back in 1999, there are still all sorts of managers who just don't get it. We've already seen that several of them fall under the classification of bully, but if that were the only way that managers acted as jerks, the problem would be relatively easy to solve.

However, there is more to marginal managers than merely being bullies. If there is a common denominator among them, it is their total lack of understanding of people. While today's best managers focus on employees as individuals and treat them with respect and trust, the managers who are off the chart on the jerk scale are totally clueless in this arena and in most other arenas as well.

There are managers who dictate, slack off, make outrageous requests or demands, and totally ignore the needs of their people. One surprising aspect of their approach to work is that most of these managers believe they are managing very well. They utilize managerial techniques and interpersonal behaviors that went out of fashion eons ago, and continue do so in spite of the vast array of problems that they cause.

These managers are actually able to motivate their employees. However, the problem is that they typically motivate them to quit. Employees under their charge repeatedly show elevated levels of dissatisfaction, absenteeism, turnover, and even sabotage, but such managers are quick to look everywhere but at themselves when trying to explain these problematic outcomes. Initially, employees will accept their managerial styles, even those that are authoritarian, arbitrary, or just plain unfair. In fact, managers who are harsh and dictatorial often generate a satisfactory level of productivity, but not for long. Given time, and not much time at that, there typically is a complete destruction of employee motivation, drive, commitment, loyalty, and productivity.

During the more than five years, it would have been nice to see a decline in the amount of e-mail regarding bosses who are behaving badly. With all of the emphasis on managerial training and development, plus the availability of a larger number of potentially excellent managers in the marketplace, one would have expected that there would have been a decrease in the volume and magnitude of dissatisfaction focused on managers. But that was not to be.

As you will see in the following sampling of letters about bosses, there are still large numbers of managers whose methods are outrageously archaic, unfair, and downright destructive. You will also see some of the more powerful strategies for dealing with them.

Pursuing trivia

Q. I have worked here for about a year in a senior management position, but my manager keeps giving me trivial projects that are better suited for a lower level position. I am reluctant to tell him for fear of looking lazy. What do you suggest I do?

A. If you want to see how many insignificant projects you can amass, then you should do just what you are doing now. By taking on these projects and doing them well, you are actually encouraging your manager to give you more.

The only way to turn off the spigot is for you to say something, and you can certainly do so without appearing to be lazy. When employees complain about the quantity of the assignments handed to them, they sound lazy; when they complain about the quality of the assignments, they sound involved.

The next time one of these little tasks comes your way, let your manager know that you are always willing to help out, but this type of project is going to interfere with several of your other key projects, and then name them. Then ask him if he wants you to change the priorities of these assignments.

Your manager's response may indicate that your so-called menial chores are not so menial, at least in his eye. If you want to continue to be the apple in that eye, you should set aside some time to complete them.

Now, what were you saying?

Q. My manager stops by my office regularly, and I give her updates on my projects and on anything else she needs to know. She says she'll get back to me, but she does not take action on what I say, and sometimes it seems she doesn't even remember what we talked about. I don't want to tell her how to manage. What do you suggest?

A. Managing by wandering around is very effective, but not if a manager's mind is wandering. Your manager probably meets with most of her team on these rounds, and by the time she returns to her office, her brain may be on overload.

You are absolutely correct in stating that you do not want to tell her how to manage. It would be ideal if she were taking some notes in her meetings with you, but that is her call, not yours.

Fortunately, there are steps you can take to increase the likelihood that she will retain your messages. The key word here, and frankly in most communications, is *redundancy*. This does not mean that you should repeat your message 10 times when you meet with her. However, using a businesslike and professional style, you can send her a follow-up note or e-mail summarizing your discussion and action plans.

This will not only serve as a prompt for her to take action, but can also serve as a listing of topics for future meetings with you. At the expense of being redundant, it is very important to emphasize how important redundancy is in the communication process.

An open door and nothing more

Q. The owner of our company has an open-door policy, but whenever any of us meet with him, he doesn't listen. He is friendly, but he always has a reason for doing things his way. Is there a way to change this?

A. There is a major difference between an open door and an open mind. For an open-door policy to have any meaning, there needs to be a true exchange of ideas.

It is very nice for the owner of your company to be friendly and accessible, but his apparent unwillingness to listen indicates that he is rather manipulative. He understands that authoritarian managers who want everything done their way often encounter overt resistance and hostility. However, by being friendly and meeting with the employees he has found that he can still have everything done his way, and the employees are more likely to acquiesce.

It sounds as though you are dealing with a paternalistic leader who believes that he knows what is best for you, whether you approve of it or not. This approach may be friendly, but it is the classical fist in the velvet glove.

In order to have any chance at having your ideas heard, you need to approach him in a sales mode. This means that you should open the discussion by having him agree with whatever you are saying, even if it is as basic as the weather.

The next step is to focus on a specific problem and the measurable way your suggestion will solve it. Be sure to use words such as "profit," "achievement," "goals," and "growth," as these will have a positive emotional charge for him as a business owner.

You should also try to use a style of speech and body language similar to his. The idea is for him to unconsciously sense that the two of you have much in common and he can trust you. If you still find resistance, tell him that you would like to use your approach on a trial basis in tandem with whatever approach is already in place. Emphasize that he can only win by this proposition.

The problem is that you are dealing with a father-knows-best leader, and even if you come up with a better way to do something, it still may be met with an open door, but not with open arms.

Another nice mess

Q. Is it possible for a manager to be too nice? Ours is very friendly and would do just about anything for us. If we make a mistake, she is patient and never gets upset. The problem is that some of the people in the department are taking advantage of her and bending the rules, and she does not realize it. She is too trusting. I'm wondering if there is a way to toughen her up.

A. It is possible for a manager to be too nice, and that's not a nice situation. On the surface, your manager demonstrates many aspects of managerial effectiveness. She is available, accessible, and communicative, and he obviously cares about the employees. The problem is that these elements do not make up the complete managerial package. To be effective, a manager also needs a back-up style that can be used in situations that require more decisive, direct, and firm leadership. Today's best leaders have that balance, but your manager does not.

Your manager actually sounds as though she is more interested in being well-liked than well-respected. In the beginning, managers who want to be well-liked quickly tend to reach that goal. However, it is not long before employees seek leadership that provides more guidance, direction, and responsiveness. Your manager's fear of upsetting the team and losing their friendship prevents her from showing these behaviors.

Your desire to toughen her up is a tough order. One approach is to advise her of the various abuses that you are seeing in the department. Her reaction is going to show you if he has a back-up style or is merely inclined to back up.

The imperfect perfectionist

Q. Our manager is a perfectionist who is intolerant of even the slightest mistakes. He can dwell on errors for days, and most of us work in constant fear of slipping up. How can we work for someone such as this?

A. The irony in your situation is that your manager is the biggest mistake of all. One of the most important managerial roles today is that of coach, and your manager is more of a tormentor than mentor.

For people to grow, mistakes are an inherent part of the process. And when an error is met with terror, employees ultimately complete only the most narrow and low-risk aspects of their jobs, and soon become dissatisfied. Your manager is taking you down this path.

In dealing with him, be sure to have a clear understanding of his expectations on each project, and devote extra effort to being as careful and accurate as possible in your work.

The next time that he is in an approachable mood, you and your associates should meet with him and let him know that your objectives are the same as his, while adding that it can be difficult to meet these objectives because of his reaction to errors. Tell him that you need his help on this problem, and leave it at that. He is the only one who can change his behavior. If you tell him how to act, you will be making a mistake.

The flight of the ego

Q. I just lost a great opportunity at work because the company changed a program that would have been assigned to me. When I mentioned my disappointment to my manager, she ignored me and started talking about a great new project that opened up for her. I got very quiet, and she said she was disappointed that I wasn't excited for her. What do I say?

A. Her comments actually merit a "huh?" from you, but there may be something better to say. The problem is that you are going through a real disappointment, and all your manager is thinking about is herself and his new opportunity.

Your manager must have a high score on the ego scale, as he seems to think he is the center of the universe, and all that really matters is whatever may be going on in his world. You have probably observed this type of behavior in previous dealings with her, although she many not have been as over-the-top as in this recent episode.

You can certainly tell her that you hope her new situation works out well. The next step is to say that you were not effusive about it because you were in the middle of a setback that you had wanted to discuss with her. Then stop and see where he goes with your comment.

If she still turns this into a conversation about herself, there is not much more you can do except hope that her new project will include a promotion or transfer.

Oh, please...

Q. I am an administrative assistant for a boss whom I cannot please. No matter what I do, he criticizes me. I listen carefully to what he wants, and then I do it, and he still says I did it wrong. When I tell him I followed his instructions, he tells me I did not understand what he was saying, but I did. I am at my wit's end. Can you suggest anything?

A. Your boss's antics are his little way of dominating you, and you have been the willing victim. He is going to continue to kick sand in your face until you draw the line in the corporate sand. The time has come for you to do just that.

On your next assignment, put everything you can in writing, and then give him a copy of your plan to tackle the work. Meet with him at frequent intervals during the life of the project to let him see that you are on track.

Sooner or later, he's going to get inappropriately critical of your work. When that happens, you should respond in a firm and businesslike way, look him squarely in the eye, and not only show him in writing that he is wrong, but tell him that his outbursts are unacceptable and have to stop right now. Then be quiet.

Sometimes people such as him need to see how far they can push others, and now he knows. That may be all he needs. But if he feels the need to start up with you, then you should start up the ladder and discuss the situation with his manager.

Are you kidding?

Q. My supervisor enjoys kidding me, and she keeps saying that her remarks are all in fun. I do not enjoy hearing her degrading comments, her repetition of the same annoying lines, and the so-called funny stories that she makes up about me. I was thinking about making some similar comments back to her and see what she thinks. What do you think?

A. When your supervisor says her kidding remarks are all in fun, she is kidding himself. The real determination as to whether remarks are in fun or are hurtful is best made by the recipient, not the sender.

It does not take much at all to turn kidding into taunting, badgering, and even inflicting distress. Her behavior raises real questions about her interpersonal skills as well as her supervisory skills.

If you try to toss some kidding remarks back at her, she will sense that you want to get into a verbal tangle with her. Her most likely reaction will be to raise the stakes and come back at you with increasingly hurtful comments, because she will want to win. This raises the most common motivation behind this type of behavior, namely, a need to sense some control and power.

The next time she starts the kidding routine, tell her, in a businesslike way, that her specific comments are hurtful and interfering with your work. Perhaps, if she senses that she has something to lose by bothering you, she will stop. If she does not get the message, then you should seriously consider taking it to her boss.

Companies can have real liability when supervisory personnel are bothering and taunting their employees. No kidding.

Oh, my words

Q. We write reports for our manager and carefully follow her guidelines, but she rewrites our work, saying that we are not giving her high quality. We think our work is fine, and she just has this thing about rewriting whatever is given to her. What should we do?

A. It sounds as though you report to a controlling manager who may be getting a little out of control. There are some managers who cannot stand anything in print unless it has their imprint.

On the one hand, it is important for a manager to maintain high standards, and this can call for some tweaking and editing of the work produced by the staff. Some managers may also do this in order to take several reports and put them into one voice for final presentation.

However, when a manager regularly rewrites the staff's work, he or she may actually be causing the staff to produce marginal work. If employees figure that whatever they write is going to be rewritten, they tend to feel that it is a waste of time to do a first-rate job.

On the next project, meet with your manager ahead and see if she would be willing on a one-time basis to try to let the bulk of your work stand as is. It will then be your job to submit an outstanding report. Her reaction is going to tell you a great deal about your future reports and reporting relationship.

The title fight

Q. I work for a medium-sized company, and I was at a meeting when one of the executive vice presidents said that there are too many inflated titles here and they should be changed to reflect more of what people are actually doing. For example, he wants to change the title of several department directors to department manager. Does this make sense?

A. Taking this type of action makes sense if the executive vice president is interested in generating dissatisfaction, ill will, and an unhealthy dose of distrust. An employee's title has a very strong psychological impact, to the point that research shows that some people are even more interested in titles than pay.

While it makes sense to have titles that are representative of the jobholders' responsibilities, there is very little to be gained by changing a title from "dire tor" to "manager," especially if the director has managers reporting to him or her. Presumably those people would then be called supervisors, and so on down the chain.

There are even compelling motivational reasons to actually use somewhat inflated titles. People feel better about having them, and they can even expect more out of themselves because they hold such titles.

The executive vice president is certainly entitled to his opinion on titles, and as new positions open up, perhaps the titles can be adjusted for the new hires. However, taking away employees' titles is a random act that is not going to have a random outcome.

No thanks

Q. I played a very important role on a redesign of our office during the past 10 months. It is finally all done and the general manager called everyone in to thank the people who worked so hard on it. I thought I would be the first one thanked, but I wasn't thanked at all. I'm very upset. What can you suggest?

A. You inadvertently worked on a thankless task, but it does not have to remain that way. When a general manager misses a golden opportunity to provide well-earned recognition to an employee, there can be any number of explanations.

Perhaps she is a preoccupied visionary who unintentionally leaves some people behind. Or maybe she was not fully aware of the critical role that you played. However, it is possible, although unlikely, that she is sending you a message.

The best way to find out is to meet with her as soon as possible. Be businesslike, direct, and honest, and tell her that you worked very hard on this project and you were disappointed she thanked everyone but you. The next step is to be quiet.

You are likely to hear a huge apology and an avalanche of thanks, but you might not. Either way, listen carefully to what she says, as her words should have a major impact on your future with the company.

When you work diligently and effectively on a project, it is rewarding to have a manager who sings your praises, because most people do not enjoy being unsung heroes.

Double the trouble

Q. I get most of my assignments from my manager, but there is another manager at his level who also gives me projects and tasks. These managers are both in top level positions. Although my manager is satisfied with my work, the other manager is never happy with it, and his communications are insulting and degrading. Most of the time, he is flat-out wrong. When I show him I am right, he ignores me. I've told my manager and he does nothing about it. How should I handle this?

A. Your tale of two managers highlights the unacceptable antics of a bully combined with the non-confrontational antics of a weakling. This organizational combo plate leaves you as the odd person out, although these managers are the ones engaging in odd behaviors.

You need to do more than merely show the bully you are right and then allow him to ignore you. You need a firm and businesslike session with him where you go line-by-line over your correct actions. If you are passive or accommodating with this type of person, the message is that you are a doormat.

Let your own manager know that the projects that are coming from the bully are interfering with your work. Tell him that you could be far more productive if he would tell the bully to stop giving you further projects unless your manager himself clears them first.

Reporting to two marginal managers is the hallmark of a poorly organized company. If you meet with these managers and nothing changes in your job, you should think about a job change.

Open mouth and closed ears

Q. We report to an individual who gives the most simplistic instructions on every project. All of us have to listen to her explanation of every detail, and once she starts talking, he stops listening. We are a sharp group of employees, but she just doesn't get it. How can we get this to change?

A. It sounds as though you report to a controlling manager who is a little out of control. Her behavior may point to some insecurities rattling around deep in her personality, and she may be overcompensating for them by forcing everyone to do everything her way. Although you are not going to be able to change her personality per se, you may be able to have an impact on her behavior.

You and some of your associates should meet with her between assignments to discuss how you would prefer to handle the next project. You can tell her that you appreciate her thorough guidance, but you are all at the point where something more abbreviated will work even better.

Then let her see what's in it for her. The benefit is simple: When everyone spends less time in the explanation phase of the project, and the project still meets the stipulated standards and objectives, productivity has increased. For any rational manager, that is a good thing. If she starts to squirm, you can suggest that she give the abbreviated approach a try on just the next project.

If she agrees to any of this, the ball will then be in your court. For a little extra motivation, just think about what she will say if you drop it.

Termination trepidation

Q. I have an employee who deserves to be fired. His work is not very good, his attitude is often negative, and even his honesty is questionable. I have talked to him about the problems and documented his performance, but the problem is that I have never fired anyone and I don't feel good about putting someone out of a job. What can you suggest?

A. Although there is newfound machismo attached to trumping an employee's marginal performance with the phrase, "You're fired," most managers do not approach the prospect of firing someone with a smile and steely stare.

Today's best managers provide struggling employees with coaching, guidance, and feedback, along with clear information regarding the consequences of continued questionable performance. It sounds as though you have taken some of these steps, but your employee has not responded.

When you allow this type of situation to continue, you undermine your own effectiveness as well as that of your department. Perhaps you are overly concerned with being well-liked, or maybe it is your desire to avoid confrontation, but allowing a problem employee to continue is unfair to you, your employees, your company, and even the employee in question. You have given him every opportunity to succeed, but he has turned them all down.

By allowing a problem employee to keep his job, you are also allowing others to wonder about your managerial skills. Ironically, your reluctance to fire a marginal employee can increase the likelihood that you will be fired.

Hands-on liability

Q. I am a 27-year-old female, and I work with a senior researcher who is very well respected. The problem is that he pats me on the behind at least once a day and I can't stand it. I told a couple of other people who work here, and they said it is a cultural thing with him and it doesn't mean anything. Does that mean I can't do anything about it?

A. It may be a cultural thing, but it's also a sexual harassment thing. This is unwanted touching, and there is no cultural wildcard that gives sexual harassers a free pass, in all senses of the word.

Depending upon your working relationship with this individual, one approach is to directly tell him that this behavior has to stop now. Describe exactly what he did to you, let him know how you feel about it, and insist that it end. You should also mention that you will get additional help if it continues.

Also, look at your company's sexual harassment policy, if there is one. There should be an internal procedure to deal with this situation. Either way, if the harasser ignores your comments, you should discuss the problem with your manager or with your company's human resources representative, if there is one. In the event that you have to take further action, it will be very important to demonstrate that you reported the problem.

If you find that the situation cannot be remedied internally, your next step should be toward your state's fair employment agency.

Double trouble

Q. Our manager micromanages most of the employees and shows favoritism to a select few. Several complained about this, and the manager's immediate supervisor has spoken to him about it more than once. It stops for a week or two, then starts again. It has gotten to the point where several have quit and others are in the process of leaving. How can those left behind deal with this?

A. There are some managers who micromanage, and others who show favoritism, but your manager has gone to even greater depths to combine both hallmarks of mismanagement.

For those of you who have decided to remain on board, there are a few additional strategies to consider. First, several of you should meet with this marginal manager and show him the measurable costs of his actions, especially in terms of turnover and lost productivity. Let him see what he can personally gain by backing off and bringing more equity into his leadership style. For example, with less micromanaging, he will get more done, the team will get more done, and that can help his chances of being promoted, hopefully soon.

You should also continue to meet with his supervisor, as this at least gives you a reprieve of a week or two, and you should consider going up an additional rung on the corporate ladder. If the situation does not improve, and you find that you are truly suffering as a result, then instead of being a person who is left behind, maybe you should be a person who has left.

Bottom fishing

Q. In reviewing one of the managers, we noticed her tendency to terminate the better employees in her department, and keep many of the plodders. We have some different theories as to what might be behind this, but we are interested to know your thoughts on it.

A. While there are a few key theories that may explain this type of behavior, the reality is that this behavior is destructive in every sense of the word. When a manager keeps the slugs and terminates all but a fraction of the sluggers, it is just a matter of time before the whole department slips to the lowest common denominator.

This managerial practice sends a clear message to the team: Do a mediocre job or you will be on the exit ramp. It also causes employees to view the company as being unfair, inconsistent, and rather mean-spirited. This is no way to generate loyalty and commitment. But it can be a very good way to generate some legal claims, such as wrongful termination.

As for the theories behind this behavior, you are most likely looking at a manager who is at least one of the following: incredibly incompetent, incredibly insecure, or incredibly political. And unless you take action to deal with her, you are going to face an incredible mess.

A fearful manager

Q. Our manager tells us that fear is a great motivator. He threatens to write us up, give us poor reviews, hold back our raises, and terminate those who are not up to his standards. I don't think fear is a great motivator at all, but I am working hard. Does he have something?

A. The only thing that your manager has is an incredible lack of understanding of management. Certainly, fear can motivate. When a manager walks into the office and threatens to terminate anyone who does not obey, the troops are going to obey, at least for a while.

The reality is that virtually every study on the effectiveness of fear as a motivator finds that its motivational impact is short term at best. It is just a matter of time before the employees start to respond with resistance, rebellion, and retaliation. Your manager has totally missed the concept of treating the employees as individuals and trying to link their needs and objectives to departmental or organizational objectives, and this is at the heart of motivation.

As a footnote, because employees tend to learn many of their managerial skills from their prior managers, it will be particularly important for you to avoid emulating this manager's style. Using fear as a motivator can be effective on a short-term basis, but it is ultimately most effective in motivating people to leave.

Pushing paper

Q. I am in sales and our company just implemented a new system that requires us to complete a huge amount of paperwork. We don't see the value of most of it, but our manager tells us that it will improve our efficiency. When we complained, she made it very clear that the paperwork has to be completed. How does this sound to you?

A. In a word, this sounds inefficient. Although documentation is important, it is difficult to consider increased efficiency and increased paperwork in the same sentence. In fact, increased efficiency of salespeople is more typically associated with a reduction in paperwork.

It is also remarkable that management implemented this change without any inputs or suggestions from you and the rest of the sales team. If management really wants to know how to increase the efficiency of the salespeople, they should ask the salespeople. What a concept!

At this point, rather than complaining about management's desire to bury you in paperwork, you and your associates should come up with some specific ways to streamline the paperwork. There are many high-tech solutions that can quickly and easily provide management with the full range of sales data, and most require no paperwork at all.

The next step is to meet with your manager, and with senior management, if necessary. Be sure to approach these meetings as sales sessions rather than gripe sessions. If management does not buy what you are saying, then it is apparent that you are now working for a company that is more interested in the volume of paperwork than in the volume of sales.

You've got to give him credit

Q. I wrote a report for management, and I asked my direct manager to have a look at it before submitting it. I am shocked and angry that he removed my name and put his on it. I did not say anything at the time, because I still have to work for him, but what can I do?

It sounds as though your boss is more skilled at writing his own name than writing the actual reports that bear it. However, before barging into his office and demanding that this outrageous breach be undone, there are some other elements to consider.

For example, there can be departmental projects that, from the outset, are delegated to the staff with the clear stipulation that they will go to the intended recipient under the department manager's signature. Some departments may even have a standard operating procedure wherein reports come from the department itself rather than from specific individuals within it. In addition, there are situations where managers take the reports prepared by their staff, make some key revisions, and submit them under their own name.

At the very least, all of this must be clarified with the employees at the outset. Anything short of that is deceitful, unethical, and unacceptable. If your boss has simply usurped your work and passed it off as his own, that is wrong. And it would be wrong of you to say nothing about it.

You should meet with your manager, go over the situation, listen carefully to what he has to say, and then determine your next step. If he has overstepped his bounds, you may need to overstep him to resolve the matter.

Pressured by a high-pressure manager

Q. I am in sales and I have been very successful with my territory. The problem is that when my new sales manager comes into town, he likes to go on sales calls with me, but then he takes over. He starts talking and even tries to close, and I don't enjoy this at all. He knows how I feel, but the problem goes on. Any suggestions?

A. It sounds as though you have a sales manager who is far more sales than manager. He still likes to get out there and mix it up with the customers, without realizing that all he is doing is getting everybody mixed up.

It makes a good deal of sense for a sales manager to go on some sales calls with the salespeople, and even to get more actively involved in the process if the salespeople are struggling. But it makes no sense at all for the manager to try to take over the sales presentation of a successful salesperson in a successful territory.

Most successful salespeople are not particularly shy, and this is no time for such behavior. You should stay in your sales mode and let your sales manager know you appreciate what he is trying to do, but clearly let him see how you feel about this. Be sure to let him see how his actions are costing him and the company money.

A sales manager should coach, guide, and support the sales team. There can be cases where the manager gets directly involved in the sales process, typically to help or to demonstrate various selling techniques. But no salesperson is going to buy the notion of a sales manager taking over the whole presentation.

Just sue me

Q. One of the managers from another department was telling me why he fired a female whom he recently hired. He said that because the department already had two females, he never should have hired a third one because women are more likely to bicker than men. He concluded by saying that he won't make that mistake again. I was dumbfounded. This guy has an MBA. Shouldn't he know better?

A. When you have found a manager such as him, your use of the word "dumbfounded" is particularly appropriate. Certainly an individual with an MBA should know better, but so should anyone who hasn't been living under a rock for the past 10 years.

With all the progress that has been made in bringing equity to the workplace, there are still many people out there who cling desperately to their old stereotypes and prejudices. Their archaic beliefs not only undermine employee motivation, productivity, and trust, they also expose the company to potential legal problems. If this manager is intent on hiring a male, regardless of the qualifications of any females who apply, that can spell real trouble.

And further, if his employees have actually been bickering, the problem may rest with his managerial skills. When there are interpersonal difficulties in a department, it makes far more sense for a manager to meet with the employees to review the situation and jointly establish a plan to correct it. Perhaps he missed this concept in his MBA program, too.

Slick tricks

Q. We report to a manager who always knows just the right thing to say. When problems develop, she calms us down and makes statements that sound as though everything is going to turn out fine. The only problem is that she is merely placating us, because she never takes care of whatever it was that got us upset in the first place. What's the best way to deal with her?

A. Managers who have the ability to say just the right thing to calm the group down, but do nothing to deal with the real issues, are typically known in the trade as "slick." Their veneer is well-polished, as is their ability to sway the group.

These managers usually have a good deal of charisma. And by using a charming and disarming style, many days can pass before the employees realize that this individual's words speak louder than his actions.

One of the more effective ways to deal with a manager who is smooth around the edges is to try to turn his generalities into specifics. When you and your associates are concerned about a specific problem and your manager provides a high gloss response, you should respond with some questions, particularly those that start with "What," "Where," "When," and "How."

The idea behind this approach is not to challenge your manager, but to try and turn her generalities into specifics. She will probably swing into super-gloss mode and ask you how the problem should be solved. You should be ready with a polished response.

Know about "No!"

Q. My manager often gives me additional projects and assignments, and I manage to fit them in and get them done. In my last review, he said I did not complete several of the main responsibilities of my job. I told him he is right, and the reason is the extra work he gave me. He said he expects more of me, so he gave me a poor review. What should I do now?

A. The best step is for you to add a new word to your vocabulary: No. You went out of your way and assumed additional assignments to help your manager in the crunch, and all that happened is that you were crunched for doing so.

The next time he approaches you with yet another assignment, you should not automatically accept it. Rather, let him know about the projects you are currently handling, and then ask which one or ones should be set aside so that you can take on the additional work.

It is possible that when he understands what you are doing and what must be deferred in order to assume the additional work, he might shop around for someone else to do it. And if he does indicate that one of your primary projects can be set aside so that you can complete additional work, that is something to keep in mind for your next review. Unless you take these types of actions, your workload will continue to go up, and your reviews will continue to go down.

Do yourself a favor

Q. My boss is always asking me to do one favor or another for her, and none of them have anything to do with my job. It's picking up her dry cleaning, dropping off a watch to be repaired, and many more, and it's usually after work. How do I say "No" to my boss?

A. Doing a favor is supposed to be an occasional event to help out another individual who is in a pinch. Doing favors all the time is simply being used. You need to do yourself a favor and address the matter with your boss. After all, this behavior is not going to stop until you tell her that enough is enough.

This does not mean that you snap back at her harshly and say, "No!" the next time she asks you to take her car to the shop. Rather you should meet with her before she has a favor in mind and tell her that you are glad to help him out in a pinch, but the current level of errands is creating a real drain on your time and you need his help to put an end to it. Then be quiet.

Her reaction is going to determine your next action. If she doesn't get the message, you can send her a more direct one the next time she asks you to take her parakeet to the vet. Simply tell her that you cannot do it because you have other plans. It's okay to do occasional favors for your boss, but this constant "favoritism" is too much.

Chapter 5

Employees Who Still Don't Get It

Coworkers continue to be a ripe source of card-carrying jerks. There's no question that fellow employees are not necessarily good fellows at all. Whether as individuals or in groups, they are still highly capable of introducing an inconceivably wide range of aggravation, annoyance, and distress into any workplace.

It makes a great deal of sense to deal proactively with these individuals and rein in their jerky actions before they pull you and your career off course. At this point, there are a number of proven steps that can help you do so. In the broadest sense, the most effective approach is to focus on their specific behaviors, and not on their personality. You can actually change their behavior, but if you are intent on changing their personality, you should try something easier first, such as reversing the flow of the Mississippi River.

In addition, as you will see, there are still many productive ways to work with, around, through, and over these problematic individuals and the problems they create.

Depending upon the range and depth of their clueless behavior, a final option is to bring a senior level person into the loop. Hopefully this will do more than reveal another level of cluelessness.

When the cat's away

Q. I am a researcher for a publishing company, and we work flexible hours. Most people start working at 7 a.m. or 8 a.m., and the boss gets in around 9 a.m. Until he arrives, five people do absolutely nothing but gab, disturbing those who want to work. The boss is aware and does not care, but the owner is extremely frugal and would have a fit if he knew. Should we blow the whistle, or let sleeping dogs lie?

A. There's no doubt that when you literally or figurative blow a whistle, you are going to awaken sleeping dogs. Sometimes that's not the worst thing in the world to do.

The first step is to take a careful look at the way your associates' behavior is impacting you. If it is basically background noise, then you should focus on your assignments and the positive aspects of your work, and figure that your marginal coworkers will cause their own demise sooner rather than later. However, if their actions are creating work-related problems or are a major assault on your sense of what is right and fair, then you and your associates should speak up. To mix a couple of metaphors, if you are going to awaken sleeping dogs, there is safety in numbers.

When all of you discuss the problem with the owner, the best way is to focus on business issues and not personalities. For example, you can indicate that flextime is causing some productivity problems, and then provide specific examples. It should not be difficult for him to realize that it is time to check up on flextime.

The meanie

Q. I work with an individual who has a chip on his shoulder. He can go all day and not talk to the four of us who share an office with him. If he does speak to us, it is with an arrogant tone. Is there anything we should say, or just keep ignoring him?

A. The real question is whether your coworker's chip on his shoulder came from his own head (sort of a chip off the old block), or whether the chip is a result of working with four people who ignore him.

Look first at your group to see if you have formed a clique that makes him an outsider. If this is the case, his behavior may be a defensive reaction to being excluded.

However, if the four of you have honestly tried to communicate with him and include him in the group, only to be ignored or subjected to verbal venom, it is easy to conclude that you should just work around him. However, you have already found that doing so is rather unpleasant.

A different approach is to meet with him and tell him that you need his help. Let him know that you are concerned about working with him, and you would appreciate knowing what he needs in order to build a more productive working relationship.

If he picks up the cue, listen carefully to what he says; if he picks up the cue and breaks it, you should go on with your work, recognizing that you did all you could to solve the problem. However, if his actions are disrupting the productivity of the office, this is a cue that your manager should pick up.

Bad mannerisms

Q. I was discussing a project with one of my coworkers when another person from our department just walked over and started talking with her about something else. There was no "excuse me" or apology, and I was left just standing there. I can't believe the lack of manners at work. What do you say in this situation?

A. In a manner of speaking, manners in many workplaces have been tossed out with old typewriters and carbon paper. It is not as if there is anything inherently wrong with interruptions, as there can be critical situations that call for them.

While it is easy to conclude that people who barge in are inconsiderate or self-centered, interruptions are becoming increasingly common and even acceptable in certain aspects of communication. For example, you are on the phone and a call-waiting beeps in. "Oh, let me take that call." With a click, the other person is left hanging while the interruption takes priority. Or you are working online and receive an Instant Message. It's really an instant interruption, and you can be perceived as rude if you ignore it. If these interruptions are acceptable, then what about barging into a conversation?

If this happens again, you can use a friendly tone and say something such as, "I'm sorry, we're not quite finished." This is not an attack, but merely a statement of fact. Unless the interrupter has a very important message, he or she will get your message. And so will the person with whom you were speaking in the first place.

The amateur psychologist

Q. One of the people I work with fashions herself as some sort of amateur psychologist. She is constantly applying psychological labels to everything I do. Our work forces us to have frequent contact, and this is really getting in the way. What's the best way to deal with her?

A. On the one hand, you could ignore her comments, but that would mean being labeled as passive aggressive and in denial; on the other hand, you could express your annoyance with her psychobabble, but then you run the risk of being labeled as frustrated, anxious, or hostile.

Her tendency to do this is part of her personality, and this means that there is not much that you are going to be able to do about it. The best approach is to keep your interaction with her focused on work-related matters that deal with the content, timing, deadlines, and objectives of your projects. While your coworker may then claim that you are in some kind of avoidance, the only thing that you should really avoid is unnecessary communication with her.

If you find that her actions are truly interfering with the work that needs to be done, then you should consider discussing the matter with your manager. Employees who waste excessive amounts of time psyching out their coworkers may actually psych themselves right out of a job.

Middle management, not middle school

Q. I'm fairly new here, and I was making a presentation in a meeting with some of the other managers when I noticed that two of them were passing notes back and forth, and they seemed to be giggling. It was annoying, but I did not let it interrupt me. Should I say something to them?

A. The behavior of your fellow employees is so juvenile that it sounds like something that would be reported to a homeroom teacher. No matter how skilled you are at making presentations, it can be quite distracting when attendees are this rude.

Unless you enjoy antics of this sort, you should say something to both of them. In doing so, be friendly and businesslike, and be sure to focus on their behavior and not on their personalities. It is much more effective to deal with the actual note-passing, and not with such traits as rudeness or lack of consideration. When you target personality, you tend to encounter resistance and defensiveness.

Tell them that you noticed their need to communicate with each other during the meeting, and then add that their note-passing was distracting and interfering with your presentation. You can mention that you understand how busy they are and how important it is for them to maintain contact, and then let them know that you would greatly appreciate it if they would either stop or take it outside in future meetings where you are presenting.

While it is tempting to pass them a note to end all notes, hopefully your friendly and businesslike advice will suffice.

Word games

Q. How do you deal with a coworker who always uses vocabulary words that most of us don't understand? He quizzes us about their meaning, usually in front of other people, and he then gives the definition.

A. So, you sense that your associate's penchant toward garish pedantry has engendered more than a modicum of vexation. In other words, his tendency to show off his vocabulary is really annoying.

Having a broad vocabulary is definite strength in many ways, as it can help an individual think more precisely, communicate more effectively, and even sense a higher degree of self-confidence. However, simply filling one's head with a batch of impressive words and then spewing them out to impress or intimidate others typically expresses little more than personal insecurity.

You are not going to change your coworker's personality, but you can still have an impact on his behavior. You and your associates should let him know that you appreciate his vocabulary, but you do not appreciate the public or private vocabulary lessons. Make sure that he understands that you regard this treatment as insulting and degrading.

Perhaps he will get the message and stop playing these word games with you. If he continues, then you and your associates should have a few words with your manager about this invidious situation.

Barbs about carbs

Q. It seems that every week or so, there is another reason to have a party and a cake in my department. I am on a low-carb diet, and I have been accused of being antisocial because I do not eat any cake. What should I do about this?

A. This is one of those questions that take the cake, even if you don't. If you were truly antisocial, you would not be going to these cake-fests in the first place. Rather than antisocial, you are merely anti-carb, and you have a perfect right to take this position.

However, it will be helpful to take a second look at your behavior in these get-togethers. If you are subtle about your desire to be cake-free, then the problem truly rests with your coworkers. But if you get on a soapbox and start ranting about the perils of carb consumption, that is another story.

Assuming that you have not opted for the soapbox, you should continue to go to these parties for your coworkers, and continue to be upbeat, positive, and friendly. People who know you should have no problem understanding that your desire to avoid carbs does not mean that you desire to avoid them.

Many companies are actually trying to encourage their employees to eat healthier foods in these types of gatherings. If you ever throw one of these bashes, maybe you could alter the menu. This does not automatically mean serving kelp or tofu, but maybe serving something from your diet could be fruitful, even if you are not actually serving any fruit.

Thanks a lot

Q. I helped one of my coworkers on a project and he thanked me a couple of times and that was fine. But, he has not stopped thanking me. Just about every time he sees me, he offers a "thanks again." I told him that he doesn't have to thank me anymore, but he keeps doing it. How do I turn it off?

A. Excessive appreciation is indeed hard to appreciate. When any form of recognition is provided constantly, it loses its meaning and can easily become a source of annoyance.

You made the right move by telling this employee that he does not need to thank you any more, but it does not sound as though he truly appreciated what you are saying. When you say, "you don't need to thank me any more," it is possible for this employee to complete your thought with, "but you can if you want."

If you want him to stop doing this, you need to be more direct. This does not mean to be harsh, just businesslike. You should sit down with him and give him some specific feedback on this behavior. Tell him that you appreciate his thanks, but his tendency to provide constant and excessive thanks is simply too much of a good thing and is diluting the message he is trying to send.

If he is listening to what you are saying, he will thank you—once.

The noisemaker

Q. I work in a professional office where the work groups are separated by five-foot tall partitions. Recently a coworker was transferred to the group next to mine, and she is extremely loud and boisterous, to the point of disrupting the work of everyone around her. I asked my supervisor (who is also her supervisor) to speak to her, but he said I should do it myself. I think this is his responsibility, and I am afraid of causing tension if I talk to her. What should I do?

A. Problems on the job can come just as easily from the volume of one's coworkers as from the volume of one's work. When a loud-speaker takes up residence next to you, there are a few steps that can help move the noise from the foreground to the background.

It is apparent that your supervisor does not want to hear about this matter, at least not at this point. While you can debate the appropriateness of his response, many supervisors want their employees to try to solve problems themselves. In addition, your outspoken coworker may become even more upset if you approach your supervisor rather than approaching her first.

The best step is to meet with this coworker. Although you indicated that you are afraid of causing tension by doing so, that will only happen if you take a heavy-handed or judgmental approach.

A better approach is to tell her that you need her help. Indicate that although you understand how important it is for her to actively communicate with others, the configuration of the office makes it difficult for you to communicate and complete your work, particularly when everything she says is as loud in your area as it is in hers. In this way, you are putting the blame on the partitions and not on her, and you are subtly indicating that her conversations are not private. Conclude by telling her that you would appreciate any action she could take to help solve this matter. If her words continue to bounce off your walls, then it is time for you and your coworkers to meet with your supervisor. Give him the facts of the problem as well as some possible solutions. If he still declines to get involved, you may need to take a step up the corporate ladder to get a real hearing.

A hands-off policy

Q. I work with several other employees in a warehouse. By the end of the day, some of us have achy muscles. My question is what to do about a coworker who says he knows all about acupressure and can soothe our muscles. He comes up behind us and squeezes our shoulders and backs. Some of the employees don't mind it, but I do not and I have told him not to do this to me any more. He still tries once in a while.

A. Your co-worker may know all about acupressure, but he knows nothing about the huge liability associated with touching other people against their will. He may call it acupressure, but others may just as easily call it intimidation, bullying, sexual harassment, or even assault and battery.

And further, there are some employees who have borderline physical ailments that should only be attended to by trained medical personnel. What would happen if your finger-happy coworker goes to work on an employee's back and something goes "pop?" What if that person is suddenly unable to move?

You should immediately discuss this situation with your manager. Most managers today will quickly understand the exposure that is associated with what your coworker is doing. A failure by management to take action in this kind of situation would only increase their potential exposure.

You were absolutely right to tell this acupressure player to keep his hands off you, and management should clearly reinforce this message. At the very least, management needs to direct this individual to start handling his job responsibilities and stop handling his coworkers.

The spreader of ill will

Q. A fellow employees comes to work when she is sick. Although she claims that she just has allergies, it is not long before I catch her so-called allergies and end up missing work. I don't want to catch her colds any more.

A. When a fellow employee literally makes you sick, some of the best steps for you to take will be those that move you away from her. This does not mean that you should treat her as an infested outcast, but it does mean that you can try to be more conscious of keeping some geography between the two of you, even when you work together.

At the same time, there is absolutely nothing wrong with mentioning to her that she seems pretty sick and may fare better at home with some chicken soup. The idea is to indicate that you are concerned about her health, and you are offering a suggestion that may help. As part of this little discussion, there is also nothing wrong with telling her that you really do not want to catch her cold. This may not send her out the door, but it may help send her a message to be more careful around you.

There can be any number of reasons for her to be wedded to her job in sickness and in health. For example, perhaps she has some deep psychological needs that prevent her from missing work no matter how ill she may be. If this is the case, there is nothing you can say or do to convince her that she would be better off taking some time off. Or perhaps your company has an incentive program that rewards employees for uninterrupted attendance, and she stands to lose some significant goodies if she misses work.

Regardless, if everyone seems to be catching her "allergies," you should meet with your manager. Your department is experiencing a situation that is interfering with productivity and is often linked to accidents, mistakes, and absenteeism. For most managers, this is nothing to sneeze at. In addition, if your company has an attendance incentive program, you should mention that it might need a second opinion. Healthy companies tend to focus rewards on service, quality, and productivity.

The blame deflector

Q. There is one person I work with who has a knack of shifting the blame from himself to me every time he does something wrong. He is well liked by management, and if I ever complain, I will look like the bad guy. How do I deal with him?

A. You are talking about a person who has earned a master's degree in business manipulation. This is typically an individual who creates a scenario in which all of the topsiders love him, and if you have a problem with him, you must be the problem. The best way to deal with him is from a distance, unless you enjoy being a cobblestone in his career.

If your work situation prevents you from distancing yourself from him, there is something you can do. The first step is to document things more carefully. Write memos to yourself on the work you are doing with this person, and be sure to detail your actions, his actions, and the progress of the project itself.

In the event that he makes a mistake and then slides the blame over to your side of the table, call him on it with facts and figures. Let him see that the facts unequivocally prove that he was the direct cause of the mistake.

Be prepared for him to respond with a song and dance befitting a Broadway musical, with muddled choruses crying for actions that "we" can take. Your best move is to sit quietly. If he can upset you, he will take that to management and build an entirely different case against you. Let him know that although he caused the problem, you are more than willing to work with him to correct it—after all, the objective is still to get the job done correctly.

Once he sees that you possess sharp facts that can pierce his Teflon shield, he will be less likely to point his finger at you when management asks what happened this time. However, he will be ready to point next time, and whenever he works with you in the future. If you want to head him off, let him know that you plan to document projects with him well into the future.

While manipulators seem to be destined to manipulate, the fact is that you are not destined to be their prey.

On being badmouthed

Q. I worked on a project with one of my coworkers, and I just heard that he has been telling people that he did all the work and I did practically nothing. The truth is that we both worked hard, and I am very disappointed that he is saying this. Should I confront him or is that just lowering myself to his level?

A. Before diving into the mud with this individual, the first step is to remember that at this point you are operating on hearsay. Perhaps his comments were taken out of context, perhaps the story was exaggerated, or perhaps nothing was said at all. In a word, you should initially gather as much factual data as possible. If you find that this person has been bashing you, then it is time to say something.

Your approach should be a conversation, not a confrontation. Give him the facts of what you heard, and then ask him what happened. Perhaps there is some explanation or clarification that can put the matter to rest. However, if the first words out of his mouth are, "Who told you that?" the odds are that he engaged in precisely what he is being accused of doing.

If you determine that you were indeed a target of his mudslinging, you should indicate that you not only want an apology for yourself, you want it delivered to anyone who heard his malicious comments as well. If he refuses to do so, the next stop is your manager's office.

Slinging mud about your co-worker is lowering yourself to his level, but defending yourself is not.

The bragger

Q. A coworker of mine constantly rushes to our supervisor and brags about everything she does here, even if it's just completing the most menial chore. None of us can stand listening to her. To make matters worse, now our supervisor is telling us how wonderful she is. What should we do?

A. You are actually dealing with two separate problems: One is the bragger and the other is your receptive supervisor.

A bragger is programmed to brag. You and your coworkers should not think that you can turn her into a paragon of humility. Her need to brag about herself is coming from some needs that are well beyond anything that you need to be handling on the job. People who work with braggers often tend to adjust their own behavior, rather than trying to adjust that of the bragger. The most common adjustment is to place the bragging comments in the same category as the background noise from the air conditioner, elevator, or traffic. This keeps the bragger happy, and the rest of the staff sane.

Your supervisor appears to be a living tribute to the advertising adage that if you hear something often enough, you start to believe it. If he actually has the time to listen to her pronouncements and then take even more time to tell you how wonderful she is, there may be some serious questions about his managerial prowess.

Nonetheless, he has given you an important message in return: He is a buyer when it comes to employee announcements about themselves. If you honestly believe that your performance equals or surpasses that of your bragging associate, you should make sure that your supervisor hears your self-advertisements, too.

In making your pitch, it is best to avoid any comments about the bragger. Rather, focus on your own measurable successes on the job. This is obviously not something you should do every day, but if your supervisor is going to be using such information to help determine raises and promotions, you should make sure that you are getting enough visibility.

There is no question that promoting yourself plays an important role in getting yourself promoted.

This is not working

Q. All of us work hard, but there is one person in our department who is just plain lazy. Her work is sloppy, she is late on everything, and she causes the rest of us to fall behind. Our manager says we should take care of this ourselves, but we have met with her, and she has made no effort to improve. What should we do now?

A. This type of problem can develop when people report to an individual who has the title of manager, but not the skills. When there is an employee who is not pulling his or her weight, the manager needs to take action, unless that manager is not pulling his or her weight either.

You should meet with this coworker again, with the objective to energize her, not to criticize her. Give her specific information and examples of how her performance is interfering with work in the department, and then ask her if there is anything you can do to help her get her job done. Her response and subsequent behavior is going to help you determine your next step.

If she continues to shirk rather than work, then your next stop is your manager's office. Show your manager specific examples of problems that your coworker's performance (or lack there of) is causing, and be sure that your manager understands the steps you have already taken to deal with the problem. It will also be important to let your manager see how he or she can personally benefit by taking action to deal with this co-worker.

If your manager opts to operate with his or her head in the proverbial sand, then you should opt to go up the proverbial ladder.

The inn crowd

Q. Several of the people I work with recently started going out after work for some socializing that can take up much of the evening. I have family commitments, so I don't join them. Now it seems that all they talk about is what they did the night before. I don't enjoy it, and I'm not sure what to do.

A. Dealing with a gaggle of fellow employees who have standing reservations on the post-work party barge is never easy. Your feelings are going to be particularly heightened right now because their socializing is a recent phenomenon, meaning that the party-pack is still in the infatuation stage where everything is fresh, funny, and exciting.

But like most other stages, this, too, shall pass. It is just a matter of time before the happy-hour herd starts to develop some cliques, disagreements, and conflict, all in the context of increasingly repetitious outings. Although these festive federations typically get off to a running start, most either explode, implode, or die of boredom.

In the meantime, your best approach is to continue to do your work as diligently as possible, keeping in mind that your workload demands and responsibilities have not changed as a result of your coworkers' behavior. You still have a job to do, and so do they. Among other things, this means that there is still a need for plenty of communication with them on any number of work-related matters.

You have a unique opportunity to gain a great deal of insight into your fellow employees. They have the choice of banding and bonding with their buddies and totally excluding you, or they can socialize together and still work with you on a friendly, communicative, and businesslike basis—that coincidentally is exactly what is delineated in their job descriptions. In terms of present and future working relationships with these coworkers, it is nice to know where you stand when the chips are down, even when the chips are potato chips.

Your letter implies that there are other employees besides yourself who are not socializing after work. Do not overlook them. It would not be surprising to find that you have more in common with them than with the inn crowd.

Committed and omitted

Q. I try to volunteer for as much work and as many committees as I possible can. I enjoy doing this type of work, and I know it helps improve my marketability. Several of my fellow employees have said that I am doing this just to get in good with management, and now they hardly ever talk to me. Is there a way to deal with this?

A. If your associates choose not to associate with you because you have fully immersed yourself in the company, they have a real problem, and it is not you. Their behavior shows signs of jealousy and even self-doubt. They do not appreciate seeing you get more recognition, and yet they may feel they should be doing just what you are doing.

Employees who put forth more effort than the rest of the group often face ostracism and enmity from their coworkers. Coworkers typically feel that fellow employees who stand out make them look bad. At the same time, employees who push themselves beyond the group norms often are not highly concerned about how the group feels about them.

If you want to reopen the lines of communication with your co-workers, while continuing to engage in the additional work that is rewarding to you, the best step is to start with the leader of the group. This does not mean the person with the highest rank, but rather the individual who has the greatest influence and informal power. Perhaps the two of you have some common interests, experiences, or expectations. If you can build a friendly and positive relationship with this person, the rest of the group will follow suit.

Regardless of the outcome, you should continue exactly what you are doing, as you need to be true to yourself, even if your associates are not true to you or to themselves.

Teasing, not pleasing

Q. There is one employee here who teases everyone, and I do mean everyone, and his comments are not funny. When I tried to tease him back, he became even more insulting and would not let up. His comments are not sexual or anything of that nature. They are just obnoxious. Very few people here are bothered by this. What can I do?

A. Although you cannot script what other people say, your actions can play an important contributory role. For example, when you engaged in the repartee with this corporate buffoon, he instantly assumed that you wanted to spar with him, so he raised the stakes.

Whatever you might ultimately decide to do in dealing with this mascot, the one step to avoid is to sink to his level and get into a verbal exchange. He will want to have the last word, and, unfortunately, it will not be good-bye.

A better approach is to try to keep your contact with him to a minimum and deal with him strictly on a businesslike basis. If he sees that he cannot get you to join the joust, he is likely to become less interested in taunting you.

There are some larger questions here, such as why the company is allowing this loose cannon to bounce through the halls. Perhaps he has a specialized function that the company sorely needs, but there are at least a few employees who react to him as you do, and the fact that the company is tolerating his questionable behavior raises questions about the company itself.

The reporter

Q. What do you do about a coworker who is constantly reporting to the boss about the poor performance or behavior of the other employees? These "reports" range from exaggerations to outright lies. This person is the boss's buddy, and that makes it very hard for the employees to defend themselves.

A. When a company has this type of buddy system, it points to two main problems: one is your coworker, and the other is your boss. The first step is for you and your associates to meet with this coworker and express your dissatisfaction with his or her behavior. Be sure to emphasize that the conversation has nothing to do with the friendship with the boss, and everything to do with spying, lying, and deceit. Tell this person that it is time for the nonsense to stop, adding that you hope you do not have to take further action at a more senior level to get the problem under control.

The next step is for you and your group to meet with this boss. Tell the boss that he or she is being given inaccurate information regarding your performance and behaviors, and then present specific documentation or examples to support your claims. Be sure to indicate that the constant tattling and prattling is undermining the productivity and effectiveness of the group, while adding that if there are negative claims voiced about you or your associates in the future, you would appreciate discussing the matter.

The weak link in this organizational chain is your boss. If he continues to be enthralled with your coworker's fictional stories, perhaps it is time to tell the non-fiction version to one of the company's topsiders.

Chapter 6

Subordinates Who Still Don't Get It

Every manager has certainly had experience with jerks on his or her team. In fact, most managers will reluctantly admit that they have one or two on the team right now. In fact, they may even be the reason why the team is not functioning as a team at all.

In this age of increased emphasis on treating employees with respect and trust, it is particularly challenging to do so when encountering employees who demonstrate excessively high levels of arrogance, immaturity, dependence, and verbosity.

As a manager, it is important to know one's employees as individuals, particularly in terms of understanding their unique drives, needs, and abilities. By doing so, a manager is in a much better position to create an environment that is more satisfying and motivational for the employees, while simultaneously aligning their goals with those of the organization.

It is interesting to note that some of the problematic characteristics of employees who distinguish themselves as jerks are actually extensions of what may have been strengths at one point. For example, while arrogance does not play well in most organizations, if it is peeled back, it becomes confidence and self-assurance, highly valuable characteristics. In the same way, badgering becomes inquisitiveness, dependence becomes cooperation, and verbosity becomes communication.

This means that before literally or figuratively dismissing jerks, it makes a good deal of sense to see if there is a way to reel in some of their behaviors and convert those weaknesses back to strengths. This approach, along with several others noted in this chapter, can help managers deal with those employees who have crossed the line and entered the realm of jerkhood.

The eager reader

Q. Whenever I meet with one particular employee in my office, he keeps looking down at papers on my desk that he should not be reading. I don't want to confront or embarrass him, but I want this to stop. What do you suggest?

A. There are a few inventions that can help here, namely the file folder, manila envelope, and desk drawer. If there are papers on your desk that your employees should not be reading, they should be put away when you meet with any members of your staff.

Independent of the notion of employees trying to read whatever is on your desk, it is also a good idea to meet with employees in front of your desk if you have room for a couple of chairs. By doing so, you remove an important physical barrier and actually set the stage for more open communications.

It is also important to consider the possibility that the employee in question is not trying to read what is on your desk at all. Some employees do not prefer a great deal of eye contact, often due to cultural factors, so they tend to look down. Other employees look down as a form of deference or even fear. It might be helpful to see if you can think of any problems on the job that may be causing this employee to keep looking down. Perhaps there is more to this situation than meets the eye.

Mr. wonderful

Q. We have an employee who is very competent but very arrogant. He does a good job in outside sales, but he has alienated just about everyone who works here. What is the best way to handle this situation?

A. When dealing with employees who may be viewing the world from a pedestal, there are a number of factors to consider before taking action. In the first place, are you absolutely certain that the issue is his arrogance, rather than jealousy by the other employees? You have a successful outside salesperson, and it is possible that the employees who are not doing as well may regard his confidence and self-assurance as unbridled arrogance.

If you determine that you are dealing with a certifiably arrogant person, you have some fundamental issues to consider. For example, because he is successfully generating revenue for the company, you may sense some reluctance to take any action. And further, it is possible that his arrogance plays an important role in his high degree of sales effectiveness. However, remember that he has also shown a high degree of effectiveness in alienating just about all of your employees, and it is safe to predict that his working relationship with them is only going to deteriorate unless some action is taken.

One step is to meet with him and suggest that he do some work in "internal sales." In a word, he needs to market himself better with the other employees. In addition, although you cannot change his personality, you can certainly have an impact on some of his behaviors. Give him specific examples of actions that have caused the employees to bristle, and then give him some coaching as to more appropriate actions to take. You can also have him meet with some of your key employees to discuss their working relationship and try to jointly develop a strategy to work more productively together.

Because change can be accelerated when people have some incentive for doing so, show him the specific ways that he can be even more successful if he has the support of his fellow employees. After all, the best businesses today have a strong sense of teamwork, unity, and shared purpose. If this is what you want for your business, then this employee needs to understand that you mean business.

Analysis paralysis

Q. When I assign work to one particular employee, he tends to overanalyze it and generate tons of data that we don't need. His role is primarily one of researcher, but whenever I tell him that he is going too far, it doesn't seem to have any effect. What do you suggest?

A. As the word implies, research literally means to search again. And for many people involved in research, there is great joy in searching and searching and searching. It sounds as though you definitely have a very joyous employee.

Just as researchers should be spending a great deal of their time researching, managers should be spending a great deal of their time managing. That is the key to handling this situation.

When you assign work to this individual, there will be real problems if you turn him loose and wait to see what he digs up. Rather, the best approach is to initially provide him with a clear understanding of the parameters, focus, benchmarks, and timetables associated with the work that he is expected to complete.

Once he is into the project, it will be important for you to meet with him at various intervals to see how the work is going. At such points, if you find that he has spent too much time pouring into an area of seemingly secondary importance, do not play the role of disciplinarian. Rather, play the role of coach and provide him with an explanation as to the steps that he should have taken, along with more focused guidance as to the steps that he should be taking from this point.

Continue to meet with him frequently during the life of the project, on a scheduled as well as informal basis, and provide fine-tuning and direction as may be needed. And if you find that he is focusing his research efforts more effectively and productively, give him positive feedback for doing so. When the project is completed, be sure to meet with him and review his overall performance from a coaching perspective.

With all of this in mind, it is equally important to be sure that you are listening carefully to his reasoning for wanting to dig deeper. After all, he is a researcher, and major discoveries do not typically conform to rigid corporate timetables.

Excuse me

Q. I have an employee who often fails to meet standards and deadlines on the projects I give her, but she always has an excuse. Never once has she said that a poor outcome was her fault. I am tired of the excuses, and I am wondering how to deal with them.

A. If your employee frequently fails and then conjures up endless excuses, she actually sounds like a poor excuse for an employee. However, before reaching that conclusion, you need to do some fact-checking.

Although unlikely, it is possible that she has somehow been a victim of an outrageous set of negative coincidences that have legitimately prevented her from performing well. You should look into the excuses that she is presenting. If you find that they are seemingly legitimate, it may be time to provide her with additional guidance and support.

However, if her excuses all follow a similar questionable pattern, such as by consistently laying the blame on others, then it is time to let her know that you are not buying her excuses. You should provide her with a clear explanation of the ways that specific aspects of her performance caused the failure in question.

On future assignments, be sure she understands what is expected of her in all senses of the word, and carefully monitor her progress. It will not take long for you to see if she has opted for personal responsibility or personal irresponsibility. Once she makes her decision, you should make yours.

The badger

Q. One of the people who reports to me constantly asks me when he is going to get promoted. I don't know when or if he is going to get a promotion, and I have told him to stop asking, but he still persists. How do I get him to stop?

A. Your employee is operating under the erroneous assumption that the more you hear his promotional message, the more likely you are to buy it. This constant barrage may sell hamburgers, but it does not sell employees.

In fact, the irony is that his non-stop questions are an indicator that he is probably not ready for promotion. They tell you that he does not have much insight into the impact he has on others, and they raise questions about his communication skills and ability to listen.

While he earns high scores on the persistence scale, it is important to remember that a strength, when pushed to an extreme, can become a weakness. In his case, persistence has transformed into annoyance.

Although employees are well-advised to let management know they are interested in being promoted, they do not need to do so several times a day. Rather, they should clearly express their interests, particularly during feedback sessions, and then let their performance, demonstrate that they are ready.

The next time your employee approaches you with his favorite question, you should simply tell him the truth. You are uncertain as to when a position will open up, you appreciate his interest in being promoted, and you have taken note of it. At the same time, tell him that he is undermining his chances for promotion by his incessant questions.

On a broader basis, it may be helpful for you to consider working with him and with your other employees to create some specific performance development plans that will help them in their current positions and increase their likelihood for personal and career growth in the future.

If he still persists with his questions about being promoted, then it is important to recognize that you are dealing less with the issue of promotion, and more with the issue of an employee who is asking the same question over and over again. And this is less of a coaching issue and more of a disciplinary issue.

Superbly superstitious

Q. I manage a small department, and one of my employees is very superstitious. She seems to have a superstition for just about everything, and this is getting in the way of her work and the work of the other employees. What's the best way to approach her?

A. When you have an employee who is consumed with superstition, there is an irony because it is rather unlucky for her to be so superstitious. If her rituals were actually bringing her good luck, you would not be trying to figure out what to do with her.

There are very successful business-people who have lucky ties, avoid black cats, maneuver around ladders, and no one says much about them. In fact, when they go into their high-rise office buildings, there is usually no 13th floor.

However, when an employee is engaging in any behavior that is preventing him or her from getting the work done, or if such behaviors are interfering with the work of others, then it is time to address the matter. Because it is unlikely that you will get at whatever is causing your employee to act this way, your best approach is to focus on her specific behaviors.

You should meet with her and indicate that certain aspects of her behavior are interfering with her performance and everyone else's. Be sure to cite some examples, describe better ways to act in such situations, and let her know that you are willing to help. If her work is truly more important than her superstitions, she should hear what you are saying...knock on wood.

The whole truth or part of it?

Q. An employee who reports to me does not lie, but he tends to withhold information that I need. When problems later develop and I ask him if he knew about what was happening, he tells me that he did, but felt that it was not important to mention it to me at the time. How do I get him to give me complete information?

A. This employee is unbelievable, literally. Even if he did not technically tell a lie, and even that is debatable, there is no debating his actions. They were either designed to deceive, mislead, and misrepresent, or he is judgment-challenged.

Either way, once the bond of trust is broken between you and your employee, everything that he or she says, or in this case does not say, comes into question. This lack of trust can undercut the entire working relationship, and will ultimately destroy it.

You should sit down with this employee and walk, step-by-step, through a specific situation where he held back information that you needed. Show him exactly what he should have said, and let him know that you need absolute openness in your discussions with him. If he is unsure as to whether a particular point or issue should be mentioned, he should err on the side of communicating too much.

He also needs to understand that it is essential for him to rebuild his credibility in the company. If there are further situations where he holds back key information, the truth of the matter is that the company is not going to hold onto him.

Insufficient initiative

Q. I am director of operations, and the human resources manager reports to me. She completes the work I assign her, but shows no initiative and never comes up with projects on her own. I'm not an expert in human resources, so I don't know everything else she should be doing. What do you suggest here?

A. There are a number of steps you can take to deal with a director of human resources who is not very resourceful. Part of the problem is that she has become comfortable in a reactive role under you.

You do not have to be a human resources expert in order to successfully manage her. Because her job is to provide human resources support to the various departments in the company, a good place to start is for the two of you to meet with the department managers to find out what they need from human resources.

This can lead to specific projects in such areas as recruitment, new employee orientation, pay and benefits programs, training and development, and appraisal systems. In the future, she should deal directly with these managers to learn about their needs and then develop programs to fulfill them.

You should also meet with her to clarify your expectations, as well as to jointly establish some specific goals and deadlines. She also needs to understand the consequences of showing no initiative. If she does not get the message, perhaps she is the wrong human for the human resources position.

The commentator

Q. One of my sales reps and I were at a meeting with one of our best customers when this rep made an inappropriate comment that she thought was cute, but it made the customer bristle. I didn't say anything at the time, but I wonder if I did the right thing, and what to do now?

A. It is never a good sign when phrases such as "best customer" and "bristle" are used in the same sentence. At this point, the only way to know if you did the right thing is if your best customer has become your former customer.

There is no precise formula to follow in a sales situation where one of your associates has a judgmental eclipse. Perhaps the best way to determine if you should say something is by looking carefully at your customer's reaction to the comment.

If your customer truly bristled at your colleague's remarks, it may have been helpful for you to try to defuse the situation on the spot. This does not mean that you should have reprimanded your associate in front of the client, unless you wanted to demonstrate that you too are capable of incredibly bad judgment. Sometimes a light comment such as, "I don't think that came out the way it was intended," followed by an easy apology is all that is necessary. From that point, you can take more direct control of the meeting and keep it focused on business.

In terms of what to do now, there is nothing to discuss with the customer. The incident is over and done. However, your colleague remains an issue. She needs to be given feedback regarding her behavior, as well as guidance regarding professional interaction with customers. She also needs to understand that if she makes any more cute remarks, things will get ugly.

Insubordination indeed

Q. I have an employee who reports to me, and she can be very conde-scending and arrogant when I raise questions or issues during meetings with her, especially when people from other departments are present. I have not called her on this during the meetings, and by the time the meet-ing ends, I figure that it is old news already. How should I deal with this?

A. If you think that insubordination is old news, then it's time for you to get some new information about management. Your employee's actions are 100-percent unacceptable, and she needs to hear that message from you.

The next time she plays her condescending or arrogant cards during a meeting, one approach is to tell her immediately that her comments and tone are interfering with the meeting and must stop. The problem is that public humiliation is not exactly an enlightened form of management.

A better approach is to wait until the meeting ends and then tell her that you need to meet with her immediately. You should then clearly describe the inappropriate behaviors in the most recent meeting, as well as in others. Be sure to provide her with dates and sample comments, and let her know that such behavior is upsetting, unprofessional, and unacceptable.

The final step is to let her know the consequences associated with this behavior. Because the issue is insubordination, the outcome can be termination. There may be a place for arrogant and condescending be-haviors, but not in your place of work.

Theft season

Q. We have noticed an increase in petty theft recently. The employ-ees know that theft is grounds for immediate termination, but we're trying to figure out the reason for the increase. Could it be the economy?

A. There can be any number of reasons for employee theft, but the most likely reason in your company and many others right now is that we are in the middle of theft season. Each year in late August and early

September, so-called petty items such as pens, pencils, staplers, and notepads all go out the back door. Do you notice the theme? They are all back-to-school items.

Employees have all sorts of rationalizations for taking these items, such as by saying they never take anything else, everyone is doing it, the items are not expensive, the company has plenty of them, and it's not that big of a deal. The problem, of course, is that it is a huge deal. It's theft, pure and simple.

You are certainly right in letting the employees know that such behavior is grounds for immediate termination. Be sure that the wording you use does not send a subtle message that undercuts the significance of the problem. For example, words such as "petty theft" and "shrinkage" tend to trivialize the matter.

If the problem is serious, you may need to implement increased security measures, but the first step is to let the employees know exactly what you have found and reemphasize what will happen to those individuals who are caught. Although it's the employees' children who are returning to school, your employees may need to learn some lessons as well.

Chapter 7

Mismanagement Versus Missing Management

Today's best managers consistently demonstrate a high degree of highly accessibility, availability, two-way communication, and responsiveness. In dealing with these leaders, it is easy to find not only an open door, but an open mind as well. As a result, it is also easy to find increased levels of satisfaction, commitment, loyalty, and productivity across their teams. They typically practice one of the most highly touted managerial behaviors, namely "management by wandering around."

At the same time, there are still managers out there who seem to regard Houdini as their mentor, because so many of them know how to disappear. And when managers disappear, many positive elements disappear with them, such as employee satisfaction, trust, communication, coordination, and productivity. And when these factors go out the door with the missing manager, they are often replaced with errors, confusion, resentment, and turnover.

The idea of being a missing manager does not mean that the manager must be physically missing. There are many managers who are present at work, but for all intents and purposes might as well be on Mars. They are difficult to pin down, and if an employee is fortunate enough to catch one, such managers still typically fail to react or respond to the employees in any meaningful way.

Missing managers miss out on countless opportunities, particularly when it comes to understanding their employees as individuals, building a productive team, keeping the employees motivated, developing the employees' skills and abilities, monitoring progress, and ultimately meeting individual, departmental, and company goals.

These managers tend to succeed in one key area: they are quite successful in convincing their employees that they are jerks.

As you will see in the following examples, there is a range of proven steps to help you hook these missing managers and reopen the lines of communication and a working relationship with many of them. For those that are particularly slippery, there are also several workarounds so that you can work while they run around.

Find something to do

Q. I just joined this company and I am ready to quit. On my first day, my office was a complete mess. The computer was filled with work and junk from the previous employee, and so was the desk. My manager is still out of town, and he left no instructions for anyone here. He called in and said he'd be back in a week and told me to "keep busy." What should I do?

A. Although your manager wants you to keep busy, it will be surprising if the company can keep you at all. There is no excuse for this type of treatment. Even if there was a major emergency, your manager owed you an explanation and a back-up plan.

However, if you quit impulsively right now, you will most likely throw yourself back into the labor market, and year-end is not a great time to be shopping for a job. Be fair to yourself and at least wait until your manager returns and see if you can find any of the compelling reasons that led you to join this company in the first place.

In the meantime, you should try to get your office in shape and meet as many key people as possible. This will help you learn more about the company and whether you truly have or want a future in it. You might even find an ad hoc mentor as you travel up and down the halls.

When your manager returns, you should discuss what happened here, but try to do so through questions rather than a flood of negative comments. His answers will tell you if you selected a questionable company.

Catch me if you can

Q. Every time I need to see my manager, she says she is busy and will get back to me later. The problem is that she never does. Once in a great while, I can catch her and meet with her on the spot. If I don't get her then, I won't hear a thing. How do you deal with a manager such as this?

A. You are obviously dealing with a manager on the move, although much of her movement appears to be away from you. On the one hand, she is displaying none of the behaviors of today's best managers, particularly in terms of being available, accessible, and responsive. At the same time, and this might be a surprise, you are part of the problem.

Whenever you want to meet with her, all she has to say is that she'll get back to you, and you go away. You have rewarded her evasive behavior, so she is likely to repeat it. She may even believe that the problem or situation you would have presented to her has been solved, so there was no need for the two of you to meet. And she may apply this thinking to the future as well.

If you want to have more direct contact and communication with her, you need to be more assertive and persistent. If you just roll over, she'll roll by. The next time she says she'll get back to you, thank her and ask what time works best for her. If you can give her an idea of why a meeting with you is worth her time, she will be more likely to think that it is about time for the two of you to meet.

The brush-off

Q. I am being given the worst assignments. They are the most tedious and boring, and they offer the least opportunity for growth. When I discuss this with my manager, he brushes off my comments and says that all of the work in his department is important, and he tries to match skills with assignments. How should I deal with this?

A. The managerial brush-off is never a good sign. You are approaching your manager with a serious question, and he is responding with platitudes.

However, your first step is to look at yourself to see if you may be the source of the problem. For example, have you developed the skills necessary to complete the assignments that you seek? Or could it be that the assignments are challenging enough, but you have been through the drill so many times that you are bored with them?

If you are truly the recipient of the less-than-desirable assignments, and you honestly believe that you have the skills and abilities to carry out more challenging work, you should meet again with your manager. Rather than expressing dissatisfaction with a particular assignment, ask your manager what you specifically need to do to receive a different type of assignment. The next step is to follow his recommendations and let him know that you are doing so.

If he continues to hand you marginal assignments and platitudes, perhaps it is time to seek out a work situation that truly matches assignments with your skills.

Do it yourself

Q. We have an unpredictable employee in our department. One moment she is friendly, and the next she is very nasty. We never know how to deal with her, so we are constantly walking on eggs. We have talked to her about this, but nothing has changed. When we told our manager, he said we should work it out ourselves. How can we?

A. While your coworker may be a Jekyll and Hyde, your manager is just Hide. You and your associates approached him with a problem that you tried to resolve, and his response was to work it out and leave him out. This is not management. Nonetheless, there are some steps you can take.

First, try to determine if there is anything that you and your coworkers may be doing to bring out this employee's negative behavior. You can ask this of yourselves, and you can ask it of her as well.

You should also ask her if there is anything that you and your associates can do to help her. At the same time, let her know that you need her help to make this work situation a productive one. Try to focus on specific incidents and the ways that they could have been handled on a more businesslike basis, and be sure to avoid name-calling or labels such as "nasty." By using this approach, you are more likely to have a discussion than an argument.

If you take these steps and still feel forced to do the egg-walk, then you should return to your manager and again ask for his help. If he still passes, you should consider bypassing him.

The mythical open door

Q. Top management in our company frequently tells us how available they are, and they place major importance on their open-door policy. I went to senior management for a particular problem, and my boss blew up at me for doing this. Did I do something wrong?

A. You took advantage of the company's open-door policy, your manager blew up at you, and you want to know if you did something wrong? What's wrong with this picture?

In the first place, it is unacceptable for your manager to blow up at you, period. And, the fact that he did so after you met with senior management leads to two key points: Firstly, he is not going to be winning any gold medals in management, and, secondly, with a manager such as this, it is not surprising that you used senior management's open-door policy.

Nonetheless, it is important to note that many companies with open door policies expect the employees to try to initially resolve issues or concerns by going to their direct supervision, and use the open door policy only if they are unable to achieve satisfaction at that level. Typically, if you approach senior management with a problem that your own manager can resolve, it is reasonable to expect senior management to hear you out, while suggesting that you deal first with your manager, and then come back to senior management if the issue remains unresolved.

Because you have an exploding manager, senior management may find many employees from your department coming to them rather than to him. If this is indicative of his overall managerial skills, senior management may consider a different open door for him.

Now you see him, now you don't

Q. I was given a very demanding assignment by my manager, and it did not go well. I take responsibility for the failure, but I must say that my manager was unresponsive to my numerous attempts to communicate with him. All he said at the end was he assumed that if I took on a project, I would get it done. What do you think of this and what should I do now?

A. Rather than spending his time making assumptions about what his staff is doing, your manager should be spending his time managing, coaching, and communicating. When managers disappear and start making assumptions about their staff, it is time to start making assumptions about their managerial skills.

At this point, you and he should sit down and discuss what happened on this project. You need to hear his full evaluation of your performance, and he needs to hear your thoughts as well. Let him know about any parts of the project that you enjoyed and that went particularly well, and then tell him that you believe the overall project would have met its objectives if you had more contact and communication with him.

However, rather than dwelling on his ability to be invisible, try to focus on ways to avoid this kind of problem in the future. Your next project should include some formal benchmark dates for the two of you to meet, along with the flexibility to have additional meetings if key issues, problems, or questions arise. You can assume that anything short of this will only lead to another failure.

Can sell, but canceled

Q. I am a sales rep for a large company, and I work with a senior salesperson. He divided the territory and kept the good accounts for himself while leaving the problems and leftovers for me. We both report to a vice president who cancels every appointment I make with him. I don't want to be branded a troublemaker, but what do I do?

A. The senior salesperson mines all of the gold from your territory and the vice president ignores you, and you are worried about being branded a trouble-maker? Frankly, you are the one person who is not a trouble-maker.

Card-carrying troublemakers are people who constantly look for problems rather than solutions. By facing a problem and looking for solutions, you are quite the opposite.

The real problem is that you have bought into the myth that people who stand up for their rights are troublemakers. The fact is that by failing to stand up for your rights, all you've done is make trouble for yourself.

As soon as your territory was dissected, it would have been far more effective for you to take immediate action. In fact, any serious problem at work calls for a serious response. In such a case, you need to decide if you are going to handle the problem or if you are going to let it handle you. By letting some time slide by, it is easy to slip into the role of corporate doormat.

Fortunately, it is not too late to take some action, and it sounds as though you do not have much to lose by doing so. Because the senior salesperson is too busy with your best accounts, and the vice president has stamped "canceled" on all scheduled or future meetings with you, it is time to consider a couple of visits.

If the company has a human resources department, you should stop by. However, if this department is not particularly resourceful, you should look up the corporate ladder and visit whoever holds the position over the vice president.

Either way, your approach with these people should not be to blast anybody. The best strategy is to provide them with the specifics of your situation, and then ask for their advice as to the best way to deal with it.

By looking carefully at their action, or inaction, you will have all the advice you need to handle this situation.

Reduced responsibilities

Q. I have been a loyal employee at this company for several years, and I am now a vice president. I have a great deal of expertise that has led to many honors for the company. However, in a recent restructuring, my job responsibilities were grossly reduced. I have tried to talk to the CEO, but he will not return my calls. What do I do now?

A. Topside managers can send a message to the employees by what they say, as well as by what they do not say. When major changes are made to an individual's job, and top management applies corporate camouflage rather than communication, the handwriting has covered the wall.

However, as a long-term senior employee, you owe it to yourself and even to your company to try and have direct contact with the CEO before you consider any further action. The fact that he will not return your phone calls should not deter you. If he will not talk to you by phone, insist on meeting with him. The best corporate leaders can always find time to meet with key employees. If he cannot or will not do so, the message is clear.

In the event that you do have such a meeting, bring the CEO up to date as to your department's numerous successes and your strategies and objectives for the future. It is possible that he has been so preoccupied with the big picture that you and your department may have fallen through one of the crevices.

If you do not get this meeting, and the reconfigured job is unacceptable, it is time to discretely network with other professionals in your field. While there are often too many applicants chasing too few jobs, there are rarely too many excellent applicants. With your significant honors and stable career path, you are far more marketable than you may think. Approach the job search in the same way that you would approach a major job project. Set up a detailed plan that includes goals, priorities, strategies, and deadlines, and then work it.

For better or for worse, we are in an era where job loyalty is not highly rewarded. This does not mean that you should not be highly rewarded; it just means that you may have to go elsewhere to get your rewards.

Exit strategy

Q. A department manager who reports to me comes in later than most, leaves promptly at 5 p.m., and is out of the office a lot during the day. Other employees need to meet with him, and when they cannot find him, they come to me. When I ask him where he was, he says he was out on business, and then adds that he is a professional and does not need to account for his comings and goings. How should I handle him?

A. This manager may describe himself as a professional, but some of his actions ring of unprofessionalism. For example, professionals do not typically wait for the clock to strike 5 p.m. so that they can be the first to the parking lot. Secondly, while professional jobs typically have a great deal of autonomy, as long as you are his manager, you can require him to account for his whereabouts.

He is a department manager, and that means that a key part of his job is to be visible, available, accessible, and responsive to his employees. His behavior is not hitting any of those marks.

Part of the problem is that you have allowed him to get away with these behaviors. The first step to correct the situation is to meet with him to clarify the performance expectations and ground rules for his position. In addition, over the short term, you should tighten the reins and monitor his performance more carefully. He might not appreciate being under the spotlight, but that's just where he belongs because his performance is spotty.

Chapter 8

Who's in Charge?

If you look at some of the day-to-day antics of any number of employees, regardless of their job level, it can be unclear as to who is in charge of whom.

For example, there are managers who ignore the supervisory personnel who report to them and basically treat them as cones to be skirted on the corporate highway. When these managers want something done, they simply bypass the individuals who report to them and go directly to the staff.

Also in this mix are the coworkers who somehow think they are in charge of their peers, along with the employees who operate under the gross misconception that they are in charge of their own managers.

In any of these organizationally upsidedown or backward scenarios, the typical outcome is a combination of dissatisfaction, confusion, stress, and downright aggravation. Many employees who encounter these self-ordained sovereigns may be quick to describe them as jerks, but they are not quick in dealing with them.

Unless the bypassed, ignored, or overlooked individuals act quickly and decisively to counteract these flexing power-players, the situation only worsens. When power-grabbing employees sense that they have some control over any of their significant others or seemingly insignificant others, they hunger for more. Before the feeding frenzy gets totally out of control, there are some steps you can take to cause these ravenous employees to lose their appetites.

Do as I say

Q. My manager has suggested more than a few times that I promote one particular individual to a new position in my department. He says that she seems like an excellent employee, but she is not my first choice. How should I handle this?

A. Much depends on what the word *suggestion* means to your manager. Looking at the history of your working relationship with him, are his suggestions friendly hints or are they friendly directives?

Your best move is to meet with him to discuss the promotion. Although you can indicate that the employee he spot-lighted has some strengths, be sure to present specific data that unequivocally demonstrate that the employee you prefer is better suited for the new position. You should also have an idea of the kind of position that better suits the employee whom your manager prefers.

The fact is that you have continuous performance data on each of the employees in your department, while your manager has bits and pieces of information gathered over time. As a result, you need to fill in the blanks. Be certain that your discussion covers what is best for the company, the department, and the individuals involved. After all, is it fair to his favorite employee to promote her into a position for which she is not qualified for?

If your manager still firmly suggests that you promote his choice, it is apparent that he has other reasons for pulling strings for this individual, while simultaneously turning you into a managerial puppet. In such a case, another firm suggestion is for you to keep your options open.

Take one step backwards

Q. I am a regional manager, and I am troubled by the performance of one of the branch managers who reports to me. When I mentioned this to my manager, he told me to "step back" and let her run the branch. I don't think she's capable of doing so. What do you suggest?

A. When it comes to stepping back and letting managers manage, it sounds as though your manager needs to listen more carefully to his own advice. There is a real possibility that he has stepped into your domain and onto your toes.

However, the most appropriate first step is for you to take an honest look at your managerial style and determine whether you are managing or over-managing. If you find that you are making the majority of key decisions, while the branch manager's decisions are limited to issues such as the number of keys to duplicate, then it's fairly apparent that your style has gone over the top.

To the extent that the bulk of managerial responsibilities in her branch are now yours, the next question is, "Why?" Typically, there can be one of two answers: She is in management meltdown, or you missed the lecture on managerial delegation. If she is in a failure mode, then your actions are appropriate; and if she is not, then perhaps it is time to loosen the reins.

The broader issue is that your own manager did not discuss the matter with you. Rather, you were simply advised to step back. It would have been far more effective as well as professional for your manager to meet with you and review the overall situation at this branch. However, it is not too late to do so, particularly if you are convinced that you are using the appropriate managerial approach.

You will need to provide your manager with businesslike documentation that demonstrates that your up-close and personal style is essential at this time. If your manager agrees, the next step is for you to continue to coach and guide the branch manager, while building the "bench strength" at her branch. However, if your manager still insists that you step back, and he offers no reasonable explanation for doing so, then it's important to recognize that this position may well be a step back in your career.

Clandestine control

Q. As a manager myself, I was annoyed to learn that my manager filled an important position under me without including me in the process. When I complained, he told me that I should focus on my main work responsibilities and be thankful for his willingness to take the time to do the hiring. What should I do now?

A. Your manager's behavior is right out of lesson number one in the controlling managers' playbook. The idea is to usurp the employees' major responsibilities, and then label the employees as ingrates if they question such benevolence.

The first step is to meet with the new hire and conduct your own interview. This is not a job interview, but it is similar. The objective is to discuss this person's work history and gather some insight into his or her experience, expertise, and style. The meeting should include an opportunity for the new hire to question you, along with a discussion of the expectations and standards for the position at hand.

It is easy to have negative feelings toward the new hire because of the way he or she was brought on board, but it is not this person's fault that your manager played the control card. Remember to keep an open mind in dealing with this person, as you may have an unconscious wish to see a failure just to get back at your manager.

You also need to meet with your manager. Thank him for the time and effort that he put into the hiring process, and indicate that you agree with his comment that you should focus on your main work responsibilities. Then tell him you believe hiring key personnel is one of those responsibilities.

Give him specific information regarding the costs of his current level of involvement in this process, such as the loss of his time, undercutting your authority, and sending a questionable message to the applicant. Give him equally specific information regarding the benefits associated with placing this responsibility in your hands, such as through more productive use of his time, increased likelihood of a successful hire, and a better chance for team-building with the new hire.

Although you cannot change the personality of the controlling manager, you may be able to change his behavior in specific situations by letting him see the costs and benefits associated with his actions.

The end run

Q. I am a department head and my manager has been going around me and dealing directly with my employees. He gives them orders and assignments, and this is upsetting me and them. I asked him to stop, but he has not done so. I am not sure what to do now.

A. The first question for you to address is why your manager feels that it is perfectly acceptable to take a corporate detour around your desk.

In many cases, this type of behavior is an indicator of managerial incompetence. And this is not just garden variety incompetence, but something that has far nicer packaging. Side-stepping managers often claim that they engage in this behavior in order to facilitate communication, take faster action on important problems, deal with the troops on a one-on-one basis, and even provide better support to the person being bypassed. Such motives sound lofty, but they are typically voiced by managers who have spent too much of their time reading management books that have more pictures than text.

At the same time, some managers bypass those who report to them if the bypassed individuals are failing to perform satisfactorily. If this is the case, your manager is by-passing you as a short-term solution, and you know what the long-term solution is.

Either way, your next step is to approach him and discuss the situation. Be sure to express yourself with words that have extra significance to him as a manager. Show him specific cases in which his behavior actually undermined productivity, communication, coordination, or teamwork, and then emphasize the point that the department will operate more effectively, and he will save a good deal of his own time, if he will deal directly with you, rather than with your troops.

If he still insists on taking a detour around your desk, remember that you can take one around his.

Ready, aim...

Q. I am in a management position, and I report to a senior manager. Last week he told me that I am wasting too much time on one particular employee, and he told me to fire her. I believe she is making progress, and I don't want to terminate her. What do you suggest?

A. At various points in your career, you will have defining moments, and this is one. You need to decide whether you are a manager or a messenger. If you are truly the manager, it is your job to assess the performance and potential of your employees.

There are all kinds of problems that can develop if you terminate this employee. For example, your credibility as a manager will drop far below zero. Your employees will see that you are not running the department, and this means that they no longer need to listen to you. Because your manager treats you as a corporate doormat, it will not be long before your employees follow suit.

Speaking of suits, this type of termination could lead to a lawsuit. While there are many technicalities involved, firing the employee under these circumstances may lead to a claim of wrongful termination.

On the other hand, you will be subjecting yourself to possible disciplinary action if you refuse to carry out your manager's directive. In order to avoid this outcome, you should not simply issue a flat refusal. Rather, you should meet with your manager to discuss the matter.

In this meeting, focus initially on your employee's performance, growth, and accomplishments. It will then be helpful to present your plan to help her continue to succeed. As part of this discussion, you should then mention the possible legal liability associated with terminating her as he suggests.

On a broader basis, tell your manager that the department is far more likely to meet its objectives if you have the freedom and autonomy to manage it. Let him know that you appreciate his inputs regarding the performance of your employees, and it has always been your practice to give all of his inputs very serious consideration. If he still insists that you follow his directive, it is evident that his definition of manager is different from yours. In reality, this is a defining moment for both of you.

Can I take your order?

Q. One of the people I work with is constantly telling me what to do. She does not have more expertise, and she and I are at the same job level. I have told her that I don't appreciate the orders, but she persists. Is there a better way to deal with her?

A. When dealing with a self-appointed and self-anointed leader, you typically need to do more than say that you don't appreciate the orders. If you want to get through to a coworker who issues directives, you need a direct approach.

The next time she sends an order, use a businesslike tone and immediately tell her how you feel. Then issue a directive of your own: her orders must cease and desist. Be clear in letting her know that you are not going to follow her orders, and if she keeps dropping them on you, you are going to drop into your manager's office.

If your coworker senses the slightest possibility that you are going to follow her orders, she is going to keep issuing them. For example, you can try to ignore the orders, and this may even lead to a temporary reduction in them. The problem is that if you then happen to engage in behaviors that look as though you are following her orders, she will think that you are finally listening to her, and that means more orders.

You are not going to change the personality traits that are causing her to think she is your boss, but by acting assertively, you may be able to change her behavior. However, even that is a tall order, and a meeting with management may still be in order.

Watch your backside

Q. I have a bright and competent person who reports to me, and she shows much initiative on the job. The problem is that she infringes in my area. She calls meetings with other departments, makes decisions that should have my involvement, and is quick to tell senior management that she is on top of situations that are my responsibility. I don't want to curtail her initiative, but I don't approve of what is happening here. What do you suggest?

A. Showing initiative is one thing, but this employee sounds as if she is moving from initiative to insurrection. You are her manager, and you need to let her know what you want.

When managers fail to set the parameters for their staff, some employees slack off and try to get away with as much as possible until you pull in their reins. Other employees are going to spot the leadership void and grab as much influence and power as possible. The red flag with your employee is her tendency to run to senior management and proclaim she is on top of matters that are arguably yours. This has to stop.

You should meet with her and review all of her actions that have been over the line, and then provide her with more specific information regarding her role and responsibilities. This does not mean that you are putting her in an overly structured job, but it does mean that she is going to be doing her job, not yours.

The untouchables

Q. I manage a branch in an area where it is very difficult to find job applicants. Because my employees are so hard to replace, I have been reluctant to discipline them for relatively minor infractions. Is this type of flexibility appropriate under the circumstances?

A. The word *flexibility* implies a progressive and responsive managerial style. However, when flexibility is applied to company policy, it often takes on less flattering definitions, such as inconsistency, unfairness, or arbitrariness.

When management indicates that some rules need not be followed, the employees can hear a much broader message: The rules are written in pencil. This typically causes the employees to develop the attitude that if the policy on one infraction can be ignored, then it can be ignored on others, too.

The ultimate outcome of your flexibility is that you are placing yourself in a no-win situation. If you ignore an infraction, you are setting the stage for even more serious behaviors to be overlooked tomorrow. And if you decide to implement appropriate discipline, claims of favoritism will echo through the halls.

The fact is that many employees feel positive about having the rules enforced because it enhances their sense of safety, security, and equitable treatment. In addition, most employees are not real pleased about working with others who flaunt the rules. By taking a flexible approach to company policy, you are actually rewarding the rule-breakers and punishing the loyal and dedicated employees.

You are also assuming that enforcing the rules will cause employees to quit. If enforcement means nothing more than dishing out discipline, then turnover may well be the result. However, this need not be the case if you try to approach these employees as a coach, rather than strictly as a judge. While you would still apply the appropriate disciplinary action, you have a chance of turning some of these employees around by having two-way communication with them, giving them specific information about better ways to handle the situations that originally got them into trouble, and letting them know that you are ready to help, guide, and support them in their efforts to improve if they can make a commitment to do so.

The bottom line is that company rules should be followed; if they are out-of-date or unrealistic, they should be revised or eliminated. This is the kind of action that flexible managers take.

Hard to handle

Q. How do you deal with an employee who phrases almost every comment in a critical and condescending tone? He reports to me, but he somehow thinks that he can lecture me in department meetings and directly attack my ideas and suggestions. I have tried to work with his comments, but he seems to be getting more and more impossible to handle. Why would he be acting this way and what do you suggest?

A. This charming employee is trying to push the envelope and push you as far as possible, and you have not acted assertively to put an end to it. As a result, he is going to become increasingly impossible until he sees that he has finally hit the wall.

Employees who act this way do so for any number of reasons, often because they are compensating for some underlying insecurity. However, it will make more sense for you to focus on his behavior rather than on the deeper factors that may determine it.

The next time he goes into his condescending mode, you should meet with him in private and give him direct feedback. Describe the specific behavior, let him know your opinion of it, show him some alternative behaviors, and then let him know the consequences if he continues down the current path.

The next step is his. If he improves, be sure to give him some positive feedback. If he becomes even more troublesome, document it and let him know how difficult it is for you to keep difficult employees on board.

Who made you boss?

Q. How do you deal with an employee who keeps saying, "You should have listened to me," every time I make a decision that does not turn out well. I listen to my employees, and I try to make the best decision at the time. How should I deal with him?

A. In any relationship, when people are told what they should have done, the reaction is typically one of annoyance. Being told what you should have done is not going to help the present situation, but is likely to exacerbate the problem and generate further tension.

On the one hand, this employee may lack a few corporate graces, but perhaps he is a strong resource who could help in the decision-making process. There are certainly some decisions that can be shared among the team, and perhaps this individual could play more of a role in such cases.

At the same time, this employee may be little more than a Monday morning quarterback, and his frequent "I-told-you-so" comments may reflect his desire to undercut your authority and exert some domination and control. If you sense this to be the case, he should be given feedback on his behavior, along with encouragement to approach you with strategies that focus on the future.

By looking carefully at the full range of this individual's behavior on the job, you will be able to determine if he is a Monday morning quarterback or a backup quarterback.

Playing boss

Q. I have an employee who keeps telling me how to manage, and he likes to use management vocabulary, such as by saying that I need to have more employee empowerment. Then he offers "suggestions" about priorities, assignments, and how to do my job. How do I get him to back off?

A. Before trying to get this employee to back off or get off your back, it is important to step back and look carefully at his behavior. If he is truly spending too much time trying to do your job rather than his, then he needs to be given some specific advice as to his own job priorities, responsibilities, and objectives. He needs to understand that you are still open to his ideas and inputs, but his own work comes first.

It also sounds as if he is approaching you with an air of arrogance and elitism. If this is actually the case, you should give him some advice as to the way to present his thoughts in a more persuasive and compelling manner. He needs to understand that his style may be preventing the substance from being heard.

If you actively close the door on him, you may be inadvertently sending a message to the rest of the team that you are not receptive to their ideas, and this clearly works against effective management today. And, it plays right into what he has been telling you.

Because he is playing manager right now, he is presumably interested in becoming a real manager at some point in the future. Unless he wants that to be in the very distant future, he should listen to your "suggestions."

Boss bashing

Q. I am not sure how to handle an employee who challenges my leadership. He makes negative comments about me to the other employees, and yesterday he flat out refused to carry out an assignment that

I gave him. He has a lot of abilities and I don't want to terminate him, but I am unsure what to do.

A. In most scenarios, when an employee flat out refuses to carry out an assignment, it is not long before that employee is flat out the door. At the same time, it helps to see if there may be any mitigating factors.

The first step is to try to determine your employee's rationale behind his refusal to follow a directive. It is possible that something about the assignment may have been dangerous, unhealthful, or contrary to accepted standards or guidelines. Your employee's explanation in such a case will help you determine your next step.

However, in terms of the bigger picture, this is an employee who has tried to undermine your leadership on numerous occasions, and he apparently has no qualms about speaking maliciously about you to everyone else. This type of behavior is better known as insubordination, and it is also better known as unacceptable.

Your employee should be given some very clear counseling, as well as a clear understanding of the consequences if his antics continue. In a word, if they continue, he will not.

Chapter 9

In All Fairness

If a company's goals are focused on generating ill will, dissatisfaction, dissention, and even legal exposure, one of the best ways to do so is to treat people unfairly. This type of treatment not only causes an employee to become upset with the jerk who may be engaging in this behavior, but, if done properly, can cause an employee to become thoroughly annoyed with his or her coworkers, subordinates, work assignments, and virtually every other aspect of the job.

As if the inequitable treatment is not sufficient, many marginal managers add icing to the cake of dissention by simultaneously announcing their willingness to look into the claims of such unfairness or even to act on them, but without the slightest intention of doing so. These hollow pronouncements do little more than fuel the flames of dissatisfaction.

When employees come face to face with unfair treatment, typified by short-sighted managers who throw choice bones to the pets and scraps to everyone else, there can be an instant decline in motivation, drive, commitment, involvement, and productivity.

In some companies, inequitable treatment has been around since their inception, often emanating from the highest levels. In other companies, favoritism is sporadic and exists primarily in pockets strewn across the organizational chart.

Either way, inequitable treatment is not something that today's employees are going to quietly accept. Employees at any job level can experience it, and at this point there are many tried and true steps that can counter it very effectively.

Stereotypically speaking

Q. One of the managers from another department was telling me why he fired a female whom he recently hired. He said that because the department already had two females, he never should have hired a third one because women are more likely to bicker than men. He concluded by saying that he won't make that mistake again. I was dumbfounded. This guy has an MBA. Shouldn't he know better?

A. When you have found a manager such as him, use of the word "dumbfounded" is particularly appropriate. Certainly an individual with an MBA should not be operating on such a blatantly foolish conception about people, nor should anyone who has read a newspaper in the last 10 years.

With all the progress that has been made in bringing equity to the workplace, there are still many people out there who are firmly grasping their old stereotypes, biases, and prejudices. These archaic belief systems not only undermine motivation, productivity, commitment, and trust, they also expose the company to potential legal problems. After all, it sounds as though this manager is intent on hiring a male for this position, regardless of the qualifications of any females who apply. That can spell real trouble.

If his employees have in fact been bickering, the real problem may be his managerial skills. After all, when there are interpersonal difficulties in a department, it makes far more sense for a manager to meet with the employees to review the situation and jointly establish a plan to correct it. Perhaps the manager missed this concept in his MBA program, too.

Accused and excused

A. Over the years, I have promoted various employees, and I just promoted one who is outstanding in terms of her output, attitude, and ability to communicate. There is one longer-term employee who is now accusing me of favoritism because I did not promote her. Her work has not been great, and she knows it, and she has not pursued any supervisory training. What else can I tell her?

A. If your decision-making has in fact been based solely on merit, this employee needs to understand that favoritism does play a part in the process, but it is different from what she thinks: you favor employees who are productive, energetic, and communicative.

You provided her with feedback on her work, and that is a very important part of this process. If she is truly interested in being promoted, she should also be given specific guidance to increase the likelihood of this actually happening. Obviously, you would make no promises here. Rather, there should be agreed-upon plans for her to improve the way she handles her current work, as well as specific objectives and timetables for supervisory classes and seminars, along with additional projects and responsibilities.

It is not uncommon for employees with questionable performance to make claims about favoritism. You are about to see if she is willing to take the necessary steps to make herself more favorable.

At the top of the nitpick list

Q. My manager is always nitpicking my work and making critical comments about it. I work very hard, but it never seems to be good enough for her. She is nowhere near this tough on the other employees, and they have even said this to me. I don't want special treatment; I'm just tired of being singled out for criticism. What should I do?

A. When you are under the managerial microscope, it is typically either a good sign or something close to an exit sign. On the one hand, your manager may have high expectations of you and is willing to devote extra effort toward critiquing and improving your performance. On the other hand, your manager may be rather exasperated with your performance and may be setting the stage for a change to be made.

The first step is for you to honestly appraise your own performance. Look carefully at the accuracy of the feedback your manager has given you.

If she is way off the mark, the best approach is for you to present her with clear, accurate, and irrefutable facts on a calm and businesslike basis.

At the same time, if there is even a hint of accuracy in her critical comments, the only way to lessen such criticism is through a change in your performance. The best approach is for you to have a high degree of contact and communication with her while you are working on your projects. Get a clear understanding of what you are supposed to do at the outset, and then meet with her several times along the way in order to be certain that all of the nits have been picked.

It will also be helpful for you to do some public relations regarding your performance. If there are situations in which you can implement some of her inputs, do so and let her know about it.

To the extent that your manager senses that you are listening to her, respecting her judgment, utilizing some of her suggestions, and arguably upgrading your performance, she will be less likely to be so critical of what you are doing. However, if she still keeps giving you two thumbs down, then it's time for you to consider meeting with her manager to provide your own review of her performance.

Beware of pet

Q. One of our coworkers is the boss's pet. No matter what she does, she is never wrong. She gets everything she wants, and we don't think it's fair. How should we deal with her?

A. How do you deal with the boss's pet? Very carefully. You may well be upset with the preferable treatment she receives, but if you walk into the middle of this situation, you might just find yourself walking out of this organization.

Your boss is practicing a ridiculous form of management that has the potential to generate dissatisfaction, disruption, and serious claims of favoritism. And further, this type of behavior undercuts teamwork, productivity, loyalty, and commitment.

At the same time, it is important to look carefully at what you mean by favoritism. On the one hand, your boss may be showering this employee with favors in order to win her attention and more.

However, it is also possible that he views this individual as the most productive individual in the department, and he is focusing attention on her because he sees her focusing such a high degree of attention on her job.

The best step in this type of situation is to do the best you can in your work, savor the variety and challenge, enjoy the camaraderie of your fellow employees, and do yourself a favor by taking your mind off of favoritism.

Take your pet on vacation

Q. We report to a school principal who plays favorites. She takes certain teachers to her summer house, plays golf with them, and gives them choice assignments, schedules, and students. How should we deal with her?

A. It can be a real problem when the principal of the school is not on top of the principles of management. One tenet of effective leadership is equitable treatment of everyone, and a second is to avoid excessive socializing with the employees.

By giving certain teachers all of the plums at work, your principal is undermining teamwork, loyalty, and motivation. This type of treatment can even transfer into the classroom and undermine the quality of teaching.

In many of today's flat organizations, there can be an increase in socializing between managers and their employees after work. However, such get-togethers should be on a professional and intermittent basis, and there should not even be a hint of favoritism.

This is a situation that you and your fellow teachers need to discuss with the principal. However, if you focus on summer houses and golf, you are going to sail right into an emotional trap. Your primary emphasis should be on issues that relate specifically to the job, such as more equitable ways to make assignments, schedules, and student placement. Try to let her see how your suggestions will personally help her, such as by their possible impact on the quality of teaching and ultimately on student test scores.

If she takes no steps to improve the situation, then you should take some steps to the regional office.

We owe you one

Q. For several months, my manager had been telling me that he was most likely going to give a very desirable work assignment to me. A few days ago, he gave it to one of his pets. All my manager said to me was, "We owe you one." What do you suggest I do now?

A. On the credibility scale, "We owe you one," is right up there with, "The check is in the mail." The fact is that you are dealing with an unbelievable manager. As other choice assignments go to some of his other pets, don't be surprised to hear, "We owe you two or three or four."

If he were truly committed to keeping his commitments, he would have said more to you than some vague throwaway line. For example, if he had met with you, discussed the decision, and pointed out the kinds of specific opportunities that he will try to steer your way in the future, that would be a far better sign.

Because he did not discuss these opportunities with you, then you should discuss them with him. Meet with him and ask him to elaborate on just what it is that he owes you. Be sure to get his inputs regarding any actions that you should be taking in order to be fully qualified when such opportunities arise. As time passes, let him know about your successes.

Unfortunately, you are dealing with a manager who plays favorites, does not keep his word, and communicates marginally. You owe yourself something better than this.

Hurt by the flirt

Q. We have a female in our department who gets all sorts of favors from the manager, and the reason is that she is a big flirt. She readily admits this and says that it is too bad for the rest of us. Should we say something?

A. When you have a coworker who is flirting with a manager, and a manager who is then playing favorites, both are actually flirting with danger. These types of corporate fairy tales rarely have happy endings.

There are certainly stories of coquettish coworkers whose ways and means have carried them far. There are many more whose charms have lost their magic, and whose careers have done likewise. When the cute relationships with their managers fade, as most inevitably do, the working relationships typically evolve into hostility, discomfort, and antagonism. These are not exactly the building blocks for job satisfaction or career advancement. And employees who have relied on style over substance for many years often find that there is no substance left when they really need it.

At the same time, a manager who is foolish enough to fall for the flirtatious employee is equally vulnerable. Your manager will soon find that his favoritism is taking its toll on departmental cooperation, coordination, and communication, as well as on the respect that you and your associates have for him. Ultimately, this can take a toll on departmental productivity, and that can take a toll on your manager's career.

At this point, you should say nothing. Their actions speak louder than your words.

In the spotlight

Q. It's very apparent to everyone that our manager shows favoritism toward me. While I have no problem with this, the issue is that my friends are giving me a bad time about it. How do I handle them?

A. At some point or another during a career, in addition to having 15 minutes of fame, every employee will have fleeting minutes of favoritism. Your time has arrived, but it does not come without some baggage.

The more your manager pours praise and perks upon you, the more your friends will bristle. When it comes to friendship, remember that friends cry when you fail, and they cry when you succeed, but for very different reasons.

The reality is that you are now face-to-face with their very green jealousy. Teasing you is a way for them to vent their frustration while building their own sense of power and camaraderie.

There are a number of ways to deal with friends when this happens. Some employees in your position consciously or unwittingly engage in a form of "dumbing down" so that they will gradually fall out of favor with the manager and then be reaccepted by the group. Unless your peers are more important than your career, this is a step to avoid.

You could sit down with your friends and express your disappointment in their behavior, but there is no reason to think that a guilt launch is going to have much of an impact. If you do take this approach, be prepared to hear comments pointing to how much you have changed and how different you are now.

By showing that you are upset with their comments, you are actually rewarding your friends because that is the reaction they are seeking. A better approach is to continue to be friendly and businesslike, while totally ignoring their petty comments. By doing this, you take all the fun and satisfaction out of badgering you. And when the behavior ceases to be rewarding, the behavior itself ceases.

One important remaining question is why you are the favorite. If it is because of your stellar performance, perhaps the favoritism indicates that you are a rising star in the organization. However, if there is no logical reason for the favoritism, be on guard because it can disappear in 15 minutes.

Instant conviction

Q. One of the more vocal employees who works for me complained about me to my manager. He said I am a dictator, and morale is terrible. My manager read the riot act to me. When I tried to defend myself, he would not listen. Some of the other employees got wind of this and told my manager I am doing a good job and not to listen to the complainer. Since then, I have heard nothing from my manager. Should I let it go or say something?

A. The only thing that should be let go is your manager. His actions indicate that he lacks not only managerial skills, but common sense as well.

When a manager hears complaints about one of his or her employees, the next step should not be to start issuing warnings, reprimands, and threats. The only logical step is to investigate the matter.

Not only was your manager wrong to accuse you without knowing the facts, he was also wrong by failing to apologize after the truth came out.

You should not ignore this matter. It is obviously upsetting you, and this distress can interfere with your performance, satisfaction, and even your health. You should meet with your manager on a businesslike basis and give him all of the facts in this situation.

Be sure he understands that you would prefer to have two-way communication with him whenever he hears complaints or concerns about you, as this type of communication is critical for departmental success. There can be any number of circumstances where managers can learn from their employees, and hopefully this will be one.

The manager's ear

Q. I work with a woman who our manager really likes, and she has been complaining to him about me. He then comes to me and says that I need to try to get along better with my coworkers, but I get along fine with them. It's his little favorite who is the problem. What should I do?

A. It sounds as though your manager's little favorite is a problem, but the bigger problem is the manager himself. Not only is he showing favoritism, he is taking punitive action based on hearing one side of a story.

As a first step, you should approach his little favorite and see if there is a way to clear the air with her. Perhaps there was an incident in the past that needs some reconciling, or maybe there are some current work issues that need to be put to rest. This may help stem the flow of venom to your manager, but the prognosis is not great.

The more important step is to meet with your manager to discuss the feedback that he gave you. Tell him that you have thought about his comments and you are somewhat confused. Give him specific examples that show that you get along well with your coworkers, and then ask him for any examples that might illustrate some problems in this area. If he cannot provide any, ask him to give you such feedback whenever he sees an instance in the future.

If you find that he is still mouthing words that his little favorite has scripted, perhaps you and some of your associates should meet with his manager. After all, most senior level managers do not look favorably on favoritism.

Chapter 10

The Feedback Backlash

Feedback continues to be one of the essential building blocks in learning, growth, development, and motivation. Without it, there is no way for people to know how they are doing, where to improve, or why they may be failing or succeeding.

As important as feedback is, there are still some individuals who practically use it as a weapon. They provide their subordinates, their peers, or even their superiors with information that is il!-timed, vague, inaccurate, unfounded, opinionated, overly evaluative, and often quite mean-spirited and hurtful. By calling it "feedback," they somehow think this provides them with license to insult others.

The irony is that the people who dole out this type of drivel could actually use some real feedback themselves. They need to understand that their behavior qualifies them as jerks.

Fortunately, there are a number of steps that the recipients of faulty feedback can take in order to move the process in a more positive and constructive direction.

Playing psychologist

Q. I work with an employee who jumps from one assignment to another, never completing any. I told him that I think he has Attention

Deficit Disorder, and he became very upset with me. I was only trying to help, but he has not gotten over this. What should I do?

A. There is an important point that needs your attention: making a diagnosis of Attention Deficit Disorder is a very complex matter that is better left to professional caregivers. While it is possible that your coworker indeed suffers from attention deficit disorder, he could just as easily be overwhelmed by his job responsibilities, absorbed with personal or family problems, or even suffering from substance abuse.

When you see a fellow employee truly struggling on the job, you can suggest that he or she consider getting some help. Some companies have employee assistance programs or a human resources specialist who can provide help or referrals.

It is also possible that although your coworker is jumping from one project to another, it may only appear that he is not completing any. After all, if he is truly getting nothing done, his manager may have something different to suggest.

At this point, you should apologize and let him know that you made the comment only because you are concerned about him. On a broader basis, when it comes to giving feedback to others, it is important to avoid using labels, lest a label be cast on you, too.

No need to insult

Q. I came up with a good idea and mentioned it to my manager. She suggested I put it in writing. After a couple of weeks, she wrote a letter back to me saying the idea was useless and left her cold. I am annoyed and wonder if I should say something.

A. It actually sounds as though your *manager's* response was useless and left you cold. Regardless of any action you take, it is important to recognize at the outset that a person who writes this type of letter is not typically inclined to listen to constructive feedback.

Even if your idea was ridiculous, there is no excuse for her response. The only thing her behavior has done is generate anger and squelch the likelihood of you ever presenting another creative idea to her. As a result, she loses, the company loses, and, unfortunately, you lose.

Because you are so upset over her reaction, you should meet with her. This should not be a meeting where you evaluate her or the letter, but rather one in which you try to clarify the ground rules. Tell her that you were confused by her response to your idea, and you want to know if there is anything you should be doing in order to avoid this type of reaction in the future. Her reply will tell you if it is a good idea to continue in her department, or if it is a better idea to broaden your horizons.

A critical mass of criticism

Q. I don't know how to deal with a manager who is always criticizing my work. Every single day she is telling me that I did this or that wrong, and now, whenever I see her, I brace myself for more criticism. What should I do?

A. On a short term basis, all you can do is brace yourself for more of the same. The irony in this situation is that your manager could be criticized every single day for her criticism of you. As a managerial approach, criticism tends to generate resistance, defensiveness, and dissatisfaction, and does nothing to correct the mistakes at hand. When employees are struggling, effective managers coach, counsel, and teach.

One step that may change her behavior starts with a careful look at your performance. Although it is normal for an employee to make mistakes along the way, if you are actually making key errors every day, you should ask yourself if you are doing everything in your power to be a highly effective employee, such as by taking courses and doing some studying. After all, the best way to reduce your manager's criticism is for you to make fewer errors.

In addition, the next time she criticizes your work, ask her for some specific guidance in order to prevent the problem in the future, and then be sure to incorporate her suggestions and let her know about any positive results. By letting her see that coaching is far more productive than criticizing, you may be able to have a positive impact on her performance as well as yours.

Name calling

Q. We were having a staff meeting and I asked a basic question. After the meeting, my manager told me that he didn't want to embarrass me in front of the others, but my question was stupid. He feels he's a hero because he reprimanded me in private, but I'm annoyed over the criticism itself. What do you think?

A. In Management 101, your manager gets half credit. He gets an "A" for providing negative feedback in private, and an "F" for the feedback itself.

The best managers today adhere to the adage that there is no such thing as a stupid question. It is not as if managers should be seeking so-called stupid questions, but it is through the opportunity to ask any question that innovation and creativity are fostered.

Your manager's actions can totally extinguish the desire to think, take some mental risks, and approach problems in new and different ways. Even if you ask the most ridiculous question in the world, it is entirely possible that your question will generate some related ideas that can truly lead to more effective problem-solving. After all, some of the greatest ideas, concepts, and inventions started as arguably stupid questions.

In addition, even if your question made absolutely no sense, the way that you were treated is ultimately going to prevent your associates from asking their own risky questions, and who is to say what creative ideas may be lost forever as a result? It's time for your manager to go back to Management 101.

The data dump

Q. The other day, my manager walked into my work area and said she wanted to give me some feedback. She then took out a piece of paper and read off a list of things that I have done wrong over the past three months. This was not my formal evaluation, and I am very upset by this treatment. What should I do?

A. Feedback is essential for motivation, learning, and performance improvement, and it seems that feedback is quite necessary in your situation; however, it is your manager that needs it. The notion of taking out a laundry list of stale complaints and dumping them on an unsuspecting employee is not even mismanagement. It is non-management.

If this is how your manager provides feedback, there may well be many other gaps in her managerial skills. As a result, there will probably be several instances where you can actually help educate her and help the department at large.

You should discuss the matter with your manager, but do not criticize her. Let her know that you are definitely interested in improving the quality and quantity of your work, and you appreciate any feedback that can help you meet this objective. In this regard, be sure to add that you want to receive such feedback as close as possible to the behavior in question.

It is particularly important to meet with your manager as soon as possible. If you delay, then you are not providing prompt feedback for her questionable behavior.

Who has a bad attitude?

Q. Over the last few months, my supervisor has told me several times that I have a bad attitude. I disagree with this, and when I try to explain, she does not listen. The incidents that she uses as examples are totally out of context. How should I deal with this?

A. When employees are told that they have negative attitudes, their typical reaction is to become even more negative. This, of course, leads to further comments about their attitude, which in turns leads to further negativity. Fortunately, there are ways to stop this cycle before it carries you away.

One step is to honestly determine whether you have a negative attitude. Try to think of any behaviors in your repertoire that could be interpreted as being at odds with your supervisor. This does not have to be a major battle, but can be testy comments, cutting questions, or defensive body language.

In addition, it is time to discuss the issue with your supervisor in more detail. Tell her that if she sees situations that point to negative attitudes on your part, you would prefer to know about them and correct them at that time. Be sure that you adequately publicize your behaviors that demonstrate a positive attitude. After all, the best indicator of attitude is behavior, and it will be very important to let her see that you are not misbehaving.

On the defensive line

Q. I have an employee who gets very defensive when I give him feedback. He argues over everything I tell him. How do you deal with someone such as this?

A. When an employee prefers to play defense when you try to provide feedback, there are a few steps that can make him a better receiver.

Firstly, be sure that your feedback is as close to the questionable behavior as possible. The longer the delay, the more the incident will fade into his memory, making it all the easier to distort and deny whatever happened.

Secondly, focus your comments on specific behavior and not on labels that describe it. For example, if this individual acted carelessly on the job, the feedback should not be to tell him that he is careless. Rather, you should describe the careless behavior and briefly review the kinds of problems that it can cause.

Thirdly, ask the employee what he or she can do to prevent this kind of problem in the future. This is not the time for pie-in-the-sky comments such as, "I'll try harder." Rather, you should work with the employee to set some specific behavioral objectives and some equally specific strategies to meet them.

Your role in this process is more as a coach than an evaluator. The idea is to work with this employee to improve his performance. If he still becomes overly defensive, then it is time to give him the same kind of feedback on that behavior.

Parlor games

Q. As part of the entertainment at our year-end dinner, the company hired a handwriting analyst. She came to the table where I was sitting with my manager and several fellow employees and asked us to write our names on a sheet of paper. Then she gave some positive descriptions of everyone except me. She wondered about my energy and persistence. I don't know if my manager bought what she was saying, but he semi-jokingly said that he wants to hire her to help screen new applicants. This experience wrecked the whole evening for me, and I'm wondering if I should discuss the matter with him.

A. Just because a handwriting analyst had a less-than-flattering description of you does not mean that the handwriting is on the wall. This person was part of the evening's entertainment, and you should leave it at that. Your persistence and energy levels are best reflected by your performance on the job, rather than by someone who does not have one fact concerning your work.

Every once in a while, one hears about a company that uses handwriting analysis in the hiring process. The positive side of handwriting analysis is that it typically provides attractively-bound reports with definitive statements regarding numerous aspects of a person's personality, such as confidence, maturity, intelligence, independence, and so forth. The only problem is that there is no scientific basis behind these assertions at all.

There have been studies where the exact same handwriting samples have been sent to different handwriting analysts, and the reports from these analysts reached totally different conclusions about the personality of the writer. Handwriting analysis is interesting, intriguing, and amusing, and its role in business is just where you found it—as entertainment at a year-end dinner.

There is no reason for you to meet with your manager to discuss the comments made by this entertainer. For whatever reason, she picked up some inaccurate cues from you. Perhaps it was your attire, pattern of speech, or the way you were sitting. Although she was analyzing your handwriting, she was looking at you and trying to gather as much data as possible.

When it comes to work, handwriting content is far more important than style, parlor games belong in the parlor, and the most accurate indicator of a person's energy level is his or her behavior. Speaking of behavior, do you think a low-energy person would write a letter?

Step it up a notch

Q. I have been having difficulties with one of my employees, and I met with her on several occasions to talk about her productivity, cooperation, and attitude. I don't want to write her up because I would rather motivate her more positively than negatively. What can you suggest?

A. You have tried to motivate this employee positively, and the results have been negative. Now it is time to do more than just talk.

You should meet with her to review the specifics of her most recent questionable behavior, and then jointly establish some specific steps to improve her performance, along with some measurable goals to be met within a given time period. Let her know that you will be there to coach her along the way. She also needs to understand the consequences if she fails to show improvement.

Putting all of this in writing is not meant to be threatening. Rather, this approach has advantages for her and for the company. It gives her a clear idea of the total game plan, and if you have her sign it, you may actually increase her commitment to making a real improvement. And if you do need to take disciplinary action, you will be in a better position to do so if you have documented her performance and involved her in the plan to correct it.

You seem to be concerned about having this employee like you. That's more likely to happen if she can sense growth and accomplishment on the job.

Wishful thinking

Q. My manager is upset with the goals I set for myself this year, and I don't see the problem. The goals included increasing gross margins, cross training my employees, and reducing turnover. My manager said that these are not goals, because goals need to be specific. Are these goals or not?

A. To be specific, you have listed hopes, not goals. It is obviously a good sign that you have positive dreams about the future, but goals are much more than that.

For a goal to be more than a dream, it needs to be specific, measurable, prioritized, and backed up by an action plan to get there. For example, if you want to cross train your employees, your goal would include how many employees will be cross trained, what the training will cover, when the training will be completed, and how the results of the training will be measured and evaluated.

If you want to make some improvements in your life, whether on the job or off, it is very important to have real goals. In fact, studies through the years have consistently found that goals can have a strong motivational impact. Having challenging yet attainable goals can be truly energizing.

At this point, one of your near-term goals should be to develop some real goals for yourself.

Generalities are useless (except for this one)

Q. In my performance review, my manager said I am the weakest link in the chain and that I need to show more energy and motivation. I do not want to be terminated, but I am not sure of what to do now. What do you think?

A. Advising someone to show more energy and motivation may be useful feedback if you are a cheerleader, but it is definitely skimpy advice when applied to more conventional jobs.

You should meet with your manager to get a clear picture of the specific behaviors that point to questionable energy and motivation on your part. The next step is to jointly develop a plan to make the necessary adjustments and corrections to bring your performance up to par.

This plan should include the specific steps you will take, the priorities of such steps, the anticipated timetables and deadlines, and the role to be played by your manager. You should establish some formal dates to meet with him, along with the understanding that you will be meeting with him informally at numerous points along the way.

By the way, the notion of being the weakest link in the chain is actually an outmoded concept. The more current metaphor is that an organization is more like a rope of interwoven fibers, the weakest one still cannot snap it. This raises a question about the fiber of a manager who gives skimpy feedback to an employee.

Untimely feedback

Q. My manager keeps putting off my performance review. It was due three months ago, and whenever I ask him about it, he says he'll do it soon. I don't know if he thinks I am doing a good job or not, and I'm even wondering if he is stalling because he wants to fire me. What should I do?

A. Managers who fail to provide their employees with timely reviews should have this deficiency noted when they are reviewed. Providing employees with timely performance appraisals is very important on numerous levels, especially in terms of motivation, documentation, training, and succession planning.

The fact that you do not know if you are doing a good job further highlights your manager's shortcoming. Independent of a formal appraisal, your manager should be meeting with you frequently to discuss your performance and provide coaching and guidance.

If your company has a human resources department, you should see if they can give him a push. In addition, if you have some colleagues who are in the same boat, several of you should meet with your manager to express your concerns and try to set a timetable to get these evaluations done. A final step is to ask your manger if there is anything you can do to help get your appraisal process started.

As for your fear of being fired, one could just as easily argue that if your manager wanted to terminate you, he would conduct the appraisal and use it as a means to further document poor performance.

Upsetting feedback

Q. Practically every time I come into the office, my manager tells me that I look upset. I am not, and I don't hear this from anyone else at work. Is there any significance to it?

A. One very good way to get people upset is to tell them they look upset. No matter how an employee feels, this type of comment causes many people to instantly wonder about their smile, eyes, hair, clothes, and body language, so it's off to the bathroom for a quick check with the mirror.

Presumably, your fellow employees are at least as open with you as your manager, so it is revealing that they are not giving you this type of feedback at all. This raises one question: Is there something about being in the presence of your manager that is upsetting you? You may want to think a little more about your working relationship with him, along with the possibility that you may be telegraphing some dissatisfaction in this area.

If you are unable to find anything that could be triggering this reaction from your manager, it is possible that your manager is personally upset with something, and, as a result, he is more likely to think that others are upset. There is also a possibility that he is upset with something about your work, and this is his way of expressing it.

It may be helpful for you to meet with him and tell him that you are not upset with anything at work, but that you are concerned that he thinks you are. The matter may end there, or he may give you a valuable piece of feedback about yourself or a piece of insight into him. Either way, this is nothing that should upset you.

Chapter 11

With Friends Like These...

People continue to believe that it would be nothing short of terrific to work with their friends. After all, they get along, communicate well, understand each other, and share some common interests. On a more global basis, working with friends would seem to be an effective way to build a solid, cooperative, and team-oriented workforce.

This is all certainly possible, but the reality is that working alongside friends also sets the foundation for misinterpreting problems, building cliques, unbusinesslike expectations, and emotional decision-making. None of them will do wonders for organizational success.

Working side by side with friends brings an emotional element into the workplace that can ignite any number of issues. Problems that are strictly work-related suddenly take on an emotional charge. For example, when an acquaintance at work makes a mistake that impacts a coworker, there can be a businesslike discussion and review to correct the problem. When the exact same mistake is made by a friend, there is an undercurrent of confusion, fear, mixed roles, and reluctance to say anything, all out of concern over the best way to give feedback to a friend while simultaneously keeping the friendship alive.

When working with friends, many garden variety business decisions easily transform into heavier friendship decisions. These can lead to questionable decision-making, as well as disruption of communication, discipline, teamwork, and productivity itself.

One piece of friendly advice is that when working with friends, the focus should be on the body of work, rather than on the buddies at work. Other strategies to help you deal with these friendly matters follow.

Friend versus friend

Q. My manager is about to be promoted, and he told me to apply for his job. I want the job, but one of my best friends here wants it too, and she asked me not to apply. I don't want to ruin a friendship, but I don't want to miss an opportunity. What do you suggest?

A. Your friend has put you in a very bad position because you both want the same position. You probably know already that a real friend would not act this way.

If you do not apply for this job, you are being totally unfair to yourself. In the first place, you will be losing a career opportunity that you want. You have most likely worked hard to this point, and if you do not apply for this promotion, then what was the point of all that work?

Secondly, if you do not apply for this position, you will lose stature in the eyes of your manager who suggested that you apply in the first place. If he sees you walk away from a chance to advance, he will certainly think twice about promoting you in the future.

If you want this position, go for it. Your friend should do likewise. No matter what the outcome may be, if you have a real friendship, it will survive.

If you do not apply and your friend gets the promotion, how are you going to feel when you report to her? Ironically enough, your friendship is actually less likely to survive if you give up this chance to be promoted.

Less than friends

Q. I have always tried to help my friends, and I made phone calls for two of them when they were out of work. Now they are working and I am not, but they won't lift a finger to help me. Any suggestions?

It sounds as though you indeed are a good friend, while those whom you describe as friends sound more as though they were acquaintances. They were more than willing to use your kindness and goodwill, and now show none of their own. But, perhaps they will.

Go back to them and be very clear about your situation and needs. Sometimes people are a little embarrassed and indirect when talking about finding a job, and that may have been your problem. Bring them up to date, and then ask if they can help.

It is possible they will step up to the plate and make a few calls for you, but you need to look beyond them. Networking is one of the most effective ways to find job opportunities today, and you should develop as wide a list as possible of any people who could help you. This can include family members, former colleagues, and people you may have met in community, civic, or social gatherings. Contact them and see what they can do, whether it's a referral, a call in your behalf, or even a few suggestions.

The greater your network, the greater your chances of connecting with a job. If your friends continue to ignore your requests, perhaps your expanded network can help you land a few new friends as well as a new job.

They're happy for you...sort of

Q. I was just promoted over several of my friends, and now they hardly talk to me. I thought they would be happy for me, but I was sure wrong about that. I wonder why I even tried for this promotion. What should I do?

A. Unfortunately, there are many people who sense that a step forward for their friends is a step backward for themselves. The good news is these feelings subside in time.

You are in the middle of what can be called promotion commotion. There are all sorts of initial stresses, strains, and pains for those who are promoted, as well as for those who are not. Resistance from former coworkers is a common part of the process.

People in your position often fall into the trap of missing the good old days, and some consider giving up the promotion and returning to the pack. They rationalize that they do not have what it takes to be in supervision.

Someone in your company believes that you have the wherewithal to make it as a leader, and it is important to recognize that you may not be able to make an accurate assessment for yourself until several months have passed. Don't be tempted to make this assessment in the first few days...or hours...or minutes.

Looking at your situation a little differently, would you rather be promoted over coworkers who are your friends or your enemies? Although there are some advantages in being promoted over friends, it is important to accept the fact that your friendship with your former coworkers has permanently changed. You can still be a friendly leader, but if you try to be a buddy as well as a supervisor, you will fail at both.

This is also a good time to honestly answer one question: has the promotion gone to your head? If it has, you may as well be promoted over your enemies, because that is just what they will become.

The best thing to do now is keep the lines of communication open with the troops and let them see the qualities they valued in you as a friend: Your openness, fairness, responsiveness, and concern for them. Many of the traits that made you a good friend are the same ones that can help make you a good leader.

The borrower

Q. There is one person I work with and regard as a friend, but he is always borrowing one thing or another from me, and he rarely returns them. I have a lot of regular contact with him, and I don't want to create a problem by saying no. What should I do?

A. Most people remember the Shakespearean line, "Neither a borrower, nor a lender be...." However, it is equally important to remember the very next line in this quote, "For loan oft loses both itself and friend...." The bottom line is that if you want to keep your friend and your things, it is time to close the lending office.

If this person is really a friend, you can be honest with him. Let him know that it is upsetting to lend things to him and never see them again.

Tell him that you think he should build up his inventory of items needed for the job, and add that you are willing to help him select whatever he needs.

Part of being a friend is to help your friends develop into stronger individuals. Although it may initially seem that you are going to create a bigger problem by refusing to lend things to him, the fact is that you are going to create bigger problems if you continue to do so. You are going to become increasingly upset, and it will just be a matter of time before things burst.

Do not wait to take this action until your friend asks to borrow something. Rather, approach him now and tell him that you want to prevent a future problem. If he is a real friend, he will appreciate your efforts to help him and the friendship.

Helping you out...the door

Q. A friend of mine at work went to my boss and told him that I am having problems with part of my job, and that is just not true. I told this friend a while back that I do not enjoy all the paperwork, but that's it. She told me she went to my boss just to help me. How should I deal with this?

A. If your friend's motive was truly to help you, then her judgment is rather iffy; and, if her motive was anything else, then your friendship is rather iffy.

At this point, you need to communicate with your friend and with your boss about what happened here. As for your friend, the best step is to let her know that if she is concerned about you, she should discuss her concerns directly with you, and not with your boss. Let her see the kind of damage that her comments can cause for you as well as for the friendship.

You should mention to your boss that, yes, you are not a big fan of paperwork, but, frankly, who is? Let him know that if you sensed that the paperwork was a serious problem, you would have approached him yourself.

At the same time, as long as the paperwork issue is on the table, perhaps you can do a little homework and see if there are either some ways to streamline it or eliminate some of it altogether. There are numerous computer programs that can be particularly helpful in this arena.

As for the future, you will probably want to be more discrete in communicating with your friend, at least for a while. It should not take long for you to see if that friendship is deep or paper thin.

A grammar queen

Q. I have a friend at work who corrects my speech in front of others. I have told her that I don't appreciate it, but she keeps doing it. Yesterday, when I said, "Between you and I," she said it's, "Between you and me." I don't even think she's right about that, but it was embarrassing. What should I say to her?

A. Between you and me, this person is not such a great friend. She is right in understanding that, "Between you and I," is not grammatically correct, but she is not right about much else.

Her objective in correcting you in public certainly does not emanate from her desire to hear English spoken in its purest form. Rather, her objective is probably to make you look weak and to make herself look strong.

In order to put a stop to this behavior, you need to do more than tell her that you don't appreciate it. This situation calls for some assertiveness. The next time she goes grammatical on you, try to meet with her as soon as possible, obviously in private. Tell her that you regard her public comments as insulting and hurtful, and you want them to stop right now. Let her know that it is very hard for you to remain friends with someone who treats you this way.

If her public grammar lessons continue, then perhaps it is time for you to teach her a lesson about losing a friend.

Visceral reactions

Q. One of my friends at work recently signed up with a multi-level marketing organization and wants me to do likewise. The products seem fine, but my "gut feeling" is that this is not for me. She keeps telling me to forget about "gut feeling" and listen to the facts. The only reason I would join is that I don't want to lose a friend. What should I do?

A. It is impossible for you to lose a friend if you do not rush with open arms and phone lines to join her budding empire. The reason is that if this person is no longer friendly with you after you decline her offer, she was not really your friend in the first place, and you can't lose what you didn't have.

Your friend keeps advising you to listen to the facts, but if she really believes that, she is missing an important one herself: research has found that some of the most powerful and effective decision-makers actually rely heavily on "gut feeling."

"Gut feelin" is the result of your mind putting the present decision through a filter made up of all of your experiences over the years. The result is that you get a visceral reaction to the decision: either you can stomach it or you cannot.

This means that your experience is telling you to pass on this one, even if your friend's multi-level company has the perfect antacid to quell your nervous stomach.

At the same time, it sounds as if you have been expressing some uncertainty to your friend as to whether you will or will not join. As long as she senses that the door is even slightly open, she will keep trying to squeeze through.

The time has come to tell her that you have made a final decision—no wavering, no equivocating, and no procrastinating. You can thank her for letting you look over the opportunity, and you can honestly tell her that you hope it is successful for her...but it is not an opportunity that you wish to pursue, and you hope that she will understand. You can also tell her you hope that your friendship will continue intact.

It is said that you cannot put a price on friendship, and you are about to see if that is true.

Some sort of friend

Q. I came up with a good idea to improve the way that our department works, and I mentioned it to one of my friends here. The next thing I knew, she presented it to our manager. He thinks the idea is terrific, and now my friend is some sort of hero. What should I do?

A. The first thing to do is open the dictionary and look up the word, "friend." You are actually talking about an acquaintance, and even that is a stretch. Before your manager commissions a sculptor to make a statue of her, you need to sit down with her and have a little chat.

The best approach is to use a low-key, assertive, and businesslike style. Your opening comments should focus on her specific behavior that you found to be so questionable—namely, her taking your idea to management. The idea was yours and she had no right to do this. The next step is to tell her how you feel about her actions. Let her know that this was upsetting and stressful, and you feel hurt and betrayed.

Having set this groundwork, you should then suggest that the two of you meet with the manager to discuss the matter. Let her know that both of you will look better in the manager's eyes if you sit down with him and honestly explain what happened.

If she categorically refuses to do this, tell her that you plan to approach the manager on your own. Incidentally, if you happen to have any kind of proof that the idea was yours, let her know that you will be bringing it with you. In your meeting with the manager, one effective approach is to tell him that you have a problem at work and you would like his help in solving it. Then describe the entire incident. If he is any kind of a manager, he will start his investigation immediately.

The larger question for you is whether you are afraid to act assertively. Being assertive is not being aggressive or obnoxious; it is merely standing up for your rights and beliefs. If you don't do so, it is quite likely that there will be others who steal ideas and opportunities that are rightfully yours.

The broken confidence

Q. I was upset with one of my fellow employees, and I made a comment about her in confidence to one of my friends at work. My friend broke our trust and told her what I said. I'm very upset and don't know what to do now.

A. These days, you can take back all kinds of things, such as clothing, electronic equipment, or even a car; but you still cannot take back the spoken word. For better or worse, you are having a "learning experience." While such an experience is often a codeword for a failure, all that it means is that you failed in a particular situation, but you are not a total failure unless you repeat the behavior that brought you here in the first place.

In the meantime, there are some actions that you can take. On the preventive side, if you are ever in doubt as to whether you should say or do anything, picture how it would look on the front page of this newspaper the next day. Whether dealing with a business issue or not, Murphy's Law still applies: If something can go wrong, it will. And don't forget Murphy's Corollary: Not only will things go wrong, they will do so at the worst possible time.

As for what to do now, instead of looking at this as a bad dream, it makes far more sense to refocus things and recognize that this is a real opportunity to grow. First, take a look at yourself and try to honestly see what caused you to make the less than flattering remark about your fellow employee in the first place. By looking at what you see as a weakness in others, you stand a real chance of identifying a weakness in yourself.

Second, until you clear the air with this person, you will continue to feel uncomfortable. The best way to find relief is to seriously consider approaching her and apologizing. After all, if you're *unsatisfied* with making a mistake, the best thing to do is to correct it.

While you and this person will not necessarily bond into lifelong friends as a result, at least the heavy air of tension for both of you will be dissipated and you can put your attention where it belongs: on your work.

And at some point along the way, you may want to talk things over with your former friend.

Two against one

Q. For the past year, I have been working in a small office with one other person. We worked well together until two months ago when a new employee was brought on to join us. She befriended my coworker, and now it's the two of them against me. I am upset with both of them, and I'm not sure what to do now.

A. You are perched in the middle of two separate situations that social scientists have often found to be rather antisocial. In the first place, groups composed of three people are often noted to be particularly troublesome. While two people can work comfortably and productively together, it is not uncommon to find that groups of three soon fall into a two-against-one scenario.

Secondly, social scientists often point to increased levels of stress, tension, and aggressiveness in crowded settings. Because your office was fairly small prior to the arrival of your new coworker, the tightened working conditions are probably adding to your level of distress.

The first step is to formulate a clear picture of the amount of time that you are actually being ignored, overlooked, or excluded by your fellow employees. After all, there are times when people in any group occasionally feel that they are being left-out.

If you find that you are being left-out more than left-in, the next step is to meet with your coworkers to discuss the problem. The idea is to review the specific nstances that upset you and then suggest some ways for the three of you to work more amicably and effectively together.

This type of situation will improve in direct proportion to the amount of communication among the players. Because you are the odd person out, it will be up to you to initiate much of the dialogue in this area. At the same time, remember that the future can bring a realignment of alliances among the three of you, along with the possibility of having more employees in your cozy little department.

It is also worth remembering that management does not like situations that upset or divide the employees. If you find that your one-on-two meetings with your coworkers are having no impact, perhaps it is time for a one-on-one meeting with your manager.

Very close friends

Q. I supervise a new employee in my department, and she is single and so am I. We ran into each other outside of work and now we see a lot of each other. We have a good time together, and I don't want to end it just because the company frowns on this type of thing. Is it much of a problem if we keep our relationship quiet and keep it completely out of the workplace?

A. With your hidden smiles, lingering gazes, and the temptation to tell just one other person, it is a matter of time before your covert relationship becomes overt. Because that is inevitable, you need to step back and look at what is actually happening here.

Because you are in a personal relationship with one of your subordinates, you are probably in violation of company policy. And as much as you may try to maintain your objectivity and professional distance, it will be extremely difficult for you to be fair with this particular employee. It is not impossible to be fair, but it is highly unlikely, especially when it comes to evaluating questionable performance.

Although it is tough to see through the fog of infatuation right now, many of these relationships do not pass the test of time. And when they run out of gas, one relatively common outcome is a sexual harassment claim.

If this relationship continues, and if you also want to continue a relationship with your employer, one of you should be thinking about transferring from this department.

Chapter 12

Pros and Conflicts

Conflicts are inevitable in the workplace, regardless of the size of the work group. As soon as two people start working with each other, it does not take much for them to start working against, around, or over each other. Conflicts are found at all levels of an organization, and they can run the gamut from an unfriendly glance to a full-scale battle.

There are still experts who believe that conflict is something to be squelched at the first skirmish. In organizations that adhere to this belief, it is common to find group-think, meaningless head-bobbing, and a reluctance to take a risk, ask a question, or disagree with the party line. This is a perfect formula for designing an uncreative, undynamic, and listless marginally operating entity.

Fortunately, through the years, there has been a growing consensus that conflict can be healthy for an organization, subject to a few caveats. If conflicts are merely accepted and treated as healthy background noise, without generating any managerial attention, they can easily transform from mild disagreement to wild disagreement.

A more productive approach is to accept conflict as a normal and healthy organizational reality, while remembering that there are boundaries, acceptable ranges of behavior, and a process of conflict management to keep the conflicts open and robust, without busting the company apart. In this context, conflict can encourage thinking outside the box, individual and organizational growth, and productive changes.

Accepting the fact that conflicts among and between departments, managers, subordinates, associates, cliques, and even customers are inevitable, it is important for people at any job level to recognize that they have the power to manage many aspects of this discord. Some conflicts are clearly caused by jerks at work, but others are thwarted by an entirely different set of jerks. Between these two extremes, there exists a healthy range of conflict and an easily accessible set of strategies to deal with it.

Employees who lose it

Q. I just terminated an employee and she became very upset and hostile. She screamed at me, insulted me, and was out of control. I told her to calm down, but that only incensed her further. I am shaken by what happened here, and I wonder what to do if this happens again.

A. When people are told to calm down, the most common reaction is to heat up. If a departing employee is yelling, screaming, or out of control, you should calmly and firmly interrupt and state that unless he or she stops immediately, the discussion is over.

For most people, the storm will pass and you can finish the termination process. However, if the employee cannot or will not calm down, you should put your own safety first and walk out and get help from other managers, human resources representative, or security staff.

Another way to look at this type of situation is from the preventive standpoint. It is important to give your employees feedback, guidance, and coaching on a frequent basis. In addition, jointly establish goals with your employees, and regularly review their progress along the way. With this approach, the idea is to provide the employees with a clear idea of how they are doing, and an equally clear idea of the implications associated with continued substandard performance.

With regular communication, goal setting, feedback, and coaching, employees should perform better and you should have fewer terminations. And if you do have to fire someone, there should be no shock for them and no shocking behavior targeted at you. And, by the way, if your company has a human resources department, having one of their representatives with you during the termination session can be very resourceful.

Contrary to popular opinion

Q. I am on a taskforce that is working on longer term goals and strategies for the company, and there is one individual who has a contrary opinion to everything the rest of us agree upon. No matter what approach we take, he seems to pride himself on criticizing it and pushing for things to be done his way. How do you deal with someone such as this?

A. Contrary to popular belief, there are many circumstances where a contrarian is an important asset in group decision-making. However, a great deal depends on your contrarion. If he is simply displaying self-oriented behavior and voicing his input either to hear himself speak or to control the group, that is a real problem. An honest look at his inputs can be very telling in this regard.

The positive side of having this type of individual on the taskforce is that he can prevent the group from nodding into a state of agreement without carefully considering a broader range of options. If he is truly focused on helping the quality of decisions by the group, his comments, criticism, and suggestions can actually be a source of innovative and creative solutions.

The best step in this case is to look honestly at the group and at this individual. It is also important to remember that groups that operate without any disagreement or conflict can often point to a lack of interest, involvement, and passion on the part of the members. Disagreement in a group is often healthy, even if some disagree with this fact.

The dueling duo

Q. Most of the departments under me work well together, but there are two that do not get along. I have worked with the department managers on this problem, but to no avail. We have brought these employees together specifically to improve their working relationship, but all they do is bicker. How do we get them to work as a team?

A. When employees seem to focus more on screams than teams, the first step is to look at the departmental leadership, just as you have done.

Be sure to look for any fundamental disagreements between these leaders, as they can easily spill over and undermine cooperation.

It is also important to see if there are structural factors causing problems between these departments. For example, does the company have any competitive programs or contests that may inadvertently place these departments in conflict with each other? In this regard, it is helpful to consider some incentives for cooperation between these departments.

There is an obvious need to bring the employees together, but not in an unstructured name-calling event. Rather, there should be some formal team building exercises, and one task should be for these employees to jointly develop a listing of the difficulties between their departments, as well as to formulate and commit to a strategy to resolve them.

As a side note, some managers have food available during these types of sessions, with the theory being that employees are less likely to fight when they are being fed. This may not work in all cases, but it is definitely food for thought.

The snap decision

Q. My manager snapped at me in public and I snapped back at him. I know he's upset with me, but I'm not sure if I should let it pass and avoid turning it into a bigger issue, or if I should meet with him to discuss it. What do you think?

A. If you and your manager snapped at each other, you should definitely meet with him to discuss what happened, and make it snappy. At this point, your encounter is an open wound, and if you leave it untreated, it will only become worse.

Instead of wondering if you should meet with him, the real issue is what to say when you sit down with him. Before doing so, organize your thoughts as to what really occurred, and be prepared to deal with fact and behaviors, and not opinions and assumptions.

Open the discussion by thanking him for taking the time to meet with you. Tell him that you are most interested in working productively with him again. Walk him through the specifics of the incident, and tell him how you honestly feel. For example, if you were embarrassed or humiliated by the public reprimand, tell him. If you feel that your performance did or did not merit some negative feedback, tell him. And, if you feel that you may have overreacted by snapping back at him, tell him that, too. The fact is that you both made a mistake. He should not have reprimanded you in public, and you should not have snapped back at him in public.

Let him know that you will do all you can to perform at a level that does not merit any reprimands, while committing to demonstrate more self-control when receiving such feedback. Having made these conciliatory commitments, tell him that you and your fellow employees can be far more productive when feedback is provided in private. Ask him what he thinks, and then be quiet and listen.

If he makes a commitment in return to try to privatize the public feedback, that is a step in the right direction. However, if he cannot manage to take this small step, the fact is that he cannot manage. This does not call for a snap decision on your part, but it does have implications regarding your near-term career plans.

Politically incorrect

Q. My manager's political views are very different from mine, and I am concerned that if he finds out, my chances for promotion are going to suffer. Whenever a group of us talks politics, such as at lunch, I nod and say very little. I'm not happy about this, but I don't want to hurt my chances to advance. Is there a better way to handle this?

A. Are you in a company where the leadership is waiting to pounce on any employees whose opinions differ from the established corporate line? No matter what else may be going on in the company, you should not plan on working in any firm where a self-imposed gag order is needed for survival. If you continue on this course, it is just a matter of time before something breaks, and that probably will be you. And you will not have much fun along the way.

This means that your first step is to determine the accuracy of your perception about the company's tolerance for political views that differ from those of the topsiders. The indirect way to do this is to take a careful look at the employees who have advanced in the firm, and compare them with those who have either left the firm or had minimal upward mobility in it.

When you look at the management team, are there all kinds of varied descriptors that best depict them, or can you describe the whole bunch of them in just a few words? If they are a narrow group, your chances of success are narrower.

You can also consider taking a more direct approach to validating your perception. You don't have to stand on top of your desk and call a noon rally for your cause, but the next time you are in a political discussion, you should lose the gag, stop the nodding, and express some of your thoughts.

It will not take long for you to start receiving some signs as to whether your opinions have singled you out as an independent, confident, and self-assured individual, or as simply a troublemaker who does not fit into the corporate mold. Many progressive companies today place a premium on diversity and the vibrant, vital, and dynamic environment that it fosters. Once you determine whether your company encourages diversity or fights it, your decision will be an easy one.

Arguing again

Q. Two of my coworkers do not get along, and whenever our manager is out, which happens often, they start arguing. I don't want to be branded as a person who runs to the manager whenever there is a problem, but this situation is upsetting everyone in the office. What should I do?

A. When your coworkers would rather punch each other than punch a time clock, this is an issue that needs to be discussed with your manager. There is a real problem in your department, and any rational manager would want to know about it.

It sounds as though you are overly concerned about being branded as a corporate crier if you go to management. If it makes you more comfortable, you can certainly try to intervene and resolve the problem yourself, but remember that the battle can easily move from two combatants to three.

The better option is for you to join forces with several of your fellow employees and then meet with your manager. After all, your coworkers sound as if they are as upset with the war zone as you are.

At the core of the problem is the fact that your manager is away from the office frequently. Because the main responsibility of a manager is to manage, this is not easily accomplished from afar. When a manager is missing, the result is mismanagement.

In your meeting with the manager, you can approach the problem of the battling employees in the same way that you would discuss any other matter that is interfering with your ability to do your job. However, your less obvious message is that your department needs more regular supervision, either by the manager or by someone acting on his or her behalf.

At present, it sounds as though no one has been designated as assistant manager or acting manager, or somebody has dropped the ball. It will be important for your manager to be sure that someone is formally empowered in an acting leadership role, with full authority to oversee the department during the manager's absence.

The warring employees in your department already know how to get along—they do it whenever the manager is present. If they can act this well in front of a manager, their performance should be even more compelling in front of an acting manager.

That's just grate

Q. I do not like a particular employee who reports to me. He's doing a decent job, but his personality grates on me. How do I deal with this?

A. Nowhere in management is it required that you find the personality of every one of your employees to be charming, endearing, or magnetic. There are plenty of managers who describe some of their best employees as being terrific on the job, while adding that there is no way they could be friends. This is not a problem; it's just a fact.

Your job as a manager is not to be concerned about whether you and this employee have what it takes to become buddies. It makes far more sense to be concerned about his motivation, productivity, and overall performance on the job.

At the same time, it is important to be aware of the fact that your dislike for his personality can start to spill over and contaminate your view of his work. If you continue to focus on the aspects of his personality that grate on you, it will just be a matter of time before aspects of his job performance will grate on you, too. In fact, this may be happening already as evidenced by your statement that he is doing a "decent" job. You specifically did not say that he is doing a good job—"decent" implies that you have some concern about his work. Is it based on performance or personality?

It may be helpful for you to step back and try to figure out why his personality annoys you. There is no quick formula to use, but there are a few tracks to follow. For example, perhaps he reminds you of someone you disliked from years gone by; perhaps his personality is closer to yours than you care to admit; perhaps he conflicts with some of your stereotypes; or, perhaps you feel that he is a threat to your job security. The point is that if you can get a better focus on why he annoys you, your chances of working effectively with him increase dramatically.

It is also important to remember that your best employees need not be your best friends. In fact, you may have more problems if they are.

The final shot

Q. I just gave my supervisor notice that I have accepted an offer for another job. She said she will need to give me an exit interview before I leave. She is an impossible boss and I've waited a long time for the chance to tell her off. Because I'm never coming back, should I do it?

A. You need to look at what you can gain vs. what you can lose. On the gain side, if you launch a barrage of venom, you may unburden yourself of the deep stressful feelings that you previously had to contain.

However, when you start this attack, do you really think that your supervisor will surrender? She is more likely to launch a counter-attack, and you will be quickly drawn into a full-blown argument. So much for stress reduction.

And things are not any better if her reaction is to surrender. By offering no rebuttal, she is telling you that she is not going to waste any more time with you. You can speak your piece, stamp your feet, and wave your arms, but all you will be left with is the hollow feeling that accompanies a meaningless victory. This certainly does not reduce stress.

Although you are not coming back to this company, what you say in this interview matters immensely. It can come back to haunt you the next time you look for a job and references are taken. If your final meeting is a verbal bombardment, do not count on a positive reference, or a job offer.

If you want to quit as a winner, show that you are a class act in your exit interview. Be honest in describing what you liked and disliked about the company, and express your concerns in a factual, businesslike, and constructive manner. Your supervisor's final impression of you will be the most lasting one, and you have total control over what it will be.

The judgmental clique

Q. There is a new employee in our work group who is smart, efficient, and friendly. Most of the people I work with want nothing to do with her, but I like her. I don't want to alienate my coworkers, but I refuse to ignore her. Is there a way to reconcile this?

A. When a clique has decided that a smart, efficient, and friendly person must be avoided, one might wonder who should be avoiding whom.

One way to resolve this matter is through the leadership role that you play. If you are a leader in this group, there is a chance that your acceptance of the new employee will signal to the others that she is "okay." You should encourage them to spend more time with her.

If you are not one of the group leaders, the other approach is for you to meet with the leader and encourage him or her to be more supportive of the new person. When the clique's leader is receptive to a new person, so are the followers.

This situation may ultimately be reconciled through managerial action. Your manager may notice what is going on, or perhaps the new person will go to the manager and indicate that she is unable to meet the job expectations because of a lack of support from her coworkers, excluding you. If management gets involved, this clique is not likely to click for long.

Reacting to an overreaction

Q. One of my fellow managers charged into my office and started ranting and raving about how one of my employees made some mistakes and caused his employees to be late on our joint project. I barked back at him, and I knew immediately that was a mistake. What is the best way to handle this type of situation?

A. When managers come charging into fellow managers' offices in a rant-and-rave mode, this does not exactly qualify them for rave reviews from the American Management Association. At the same time, you are correct in thinking that it was not a great idea to get into barking contest with him.

Looking first at the actual situation, the best approach for you to take when encountering this type of verbal attack is to listen, let him recite his litany, and then take the one step that can help resolve the matter: Tell him that you will look into the situation immediately and get back to him as soon as possible. After all, when he is going through his tirade, you have no way of knowing if his facts concerning your employee are accurate or not. There is not much of a basis for a discussion or an argument until you have checked out the situation.

After you have conducted your investigation, the next step is to meet with this manager and present him with facts, documentation, and a suggested plan of correction, whether the problem was caused by your employee or not. After all, it is a joint project.

The real issue is that your two departments are dependent upon each other on various projects, but it sounds as though there has been minimal managerial communication and coordination during such projects. The best way to avoid this kind of problem in the future is for the two of you to establish a more formalized timetable that calls for both of you to meet at several points along the way to discuss progress and resolve problems before they turn into crises.

When there are surprises at the end of an interdepartmental project, they are typically symptoms of a lack of adequate managerial communication and follow-up during the life of the project. And, speaking of communication, you and your fellow manager should discuss the blow-up that occurred and commit yourselves to talk rather than rant, rave, or bark, if problems develop.

Chapter 13

Securely Dealing With Insecurity

Some of the more annoying behaviors of jerks at work continue to emanate from their own insecurities. Although many of these behaviors are designed to portray confidence, strength, and dominance, the fact that an employee feels compelled to display them merely highlights his or her underlying self-doubts.

Employees who constantly insult or downgrade their coworkers, while spending an equal amount of time placing themselves on pedestals, are merely playing out their own insecurities. Their behavior is often disruptive, destructive, and annoying, but such outcomes are not altogether unwanted by them. In fact, they are a twisted form of control.

There is no magic formula that takes these insecure individuals and turns them into Rocks of Gibraltar, because their insecurities are part of their personalities. In fact, the Rock of Gibraltar is easier to change than a personality. At the same time, there are ways to securely deal with these individuals so that their antics and actions are less likely to rock the organization.

A high degree of insecurity

Q. I presented an analysis at a recent meeting, and one of my associates said that I did a good job for a person who went to a state university. He went to a big-name school and is always reminding everyone about this. I stared at him in shock and did not say anything. I completed my summary and sat down. I think I handled this right, but is it worth saying something to him?

A. You have an associate who went to a big-name school and made a big-time fool out of himself. He probably has some big-time insecurities about himself and his personal competence and effectiveness, and the only way to bolster his shaky foundation is to play his collegiate card.

You handled this situation extremely well. It would have been easy to snap back, challenge him, or jump into an absurd argument. You took the high road on this one, and it was the right path to take. Simply staring at him in shock is a powerful way to send a compelling message.

If his comments are still bothering you, then you should let him know. Tell him that it was fun to dabble in sophomoric rivalries when you were a sophomore, but today's projects, responsibilities, and accomplishments are far more important.

Whether he gets the message or not, the truth is that every time he harkens back to his academic pedigree, he is only making himself look foolish. As in so many aspects of life, it is far wiser to focus on where we are going rather than where we have been.

The friendly insult

Q. Whenever I am at a meeting with my manager, he always has a couple of "friendly insults" about me in front of the others. I don't like this, but it is the only thing I don't enjoy about working with him. I don't feel like creating a problem, so I'm not sure what to do.

A. There is no way that you can create a problem that already exists. In fact, it even has a title: manager. Rather than worrying about causing a problem, your focus should be on devising a strategy to correct one. While it may be tempting to give your manager a good elbow every time he delivers a put-down, there is no point to adding injury to insult.

Whether you recognize it or not, he is threatened by you. It does not matter if he has any real need to be concerned about the possibility of your upstaging him, he wants to make sure that this does not happen. By his little put-downs in front of an audience, he is trying to let everyone know that he is the star, and you better not outshine him.

You implied that all other aspects of your working relationship with him are positive. If this is the case, presumably you can openly express your concerns about any aspect of work to him. In this kind of working relationship, if there were something about your performance that bothered him, no doubt he would mention it to you. In turn, now that there is something about his performance that bothers you, it is fair and appropriate for you to mention it to him.

While it's always important to voice your concerns about a particular behavior as close to an actual incident as possible, this does not mean you should launch into him at the next meeting just as he delivers what he thinks is a master insult. However, as soon as the two of you have a chance to talk and debrief after the meeting, you should tell him what you think.

Your comments should not focus on him, but rather should be directed only at the behavior that bothered you. You should be as specific as possible, let him know your feelings about it, and tell him that you want it to stop now. If he is as good a manager as you think he is, he'll get the message.

Looking good

Q. At a meeting with our manager and two members of senior management, our manager answered a question but was not very clear. When one of the senior managers asked several of us for elaboration, I provided it. Afterwards, my manager thanked me for making him look bad. Now he is very aloof. What can I do?

A. Your manager could have just as easily thanked you for making him look good. After all, you are a member of his team, and it is widely believed that strong managers hire strong employees.

Part of this issue obviously depends on the way that you elaborated on his answer. For example, if you opened by implying that your manager is some sort of a dim bulb, then his reaction is not altogether surprising.

The more likely case is that your manager is feeling insecure and may sense that you are going to leap over him. The problem in this scenario is that he may consciously or unconsciously try to place you in situations where your goals, needs, and motivations are not being met, and where you ultimately fail.

You should meet with your manager and tell him that you sense a drop in communication with him lately, and then let him talk. If he is upset with your comments at the meeting, emphasize the fact that you simply provided information on a question from senior management. Neither he nor the department would have looked better if all of you sat there and stared blankly at the senior manager. As for the future, if he expects you and your staff to dumb down in these types of situations, then it may be downright dumb to remain in this department.

Hooked on compliments

Q. How do you deal with an employee who is always fishing for compliments? I manage six people, and one is always telling me about something good that she did. After I compliment her, she is happy and goes back to work. It's getting a little tiring. Do you have any suggestions?

A. When you have an employee who is fishing for compliments, take the bait and give her the recognition she seeks. If this is what it takes to keep her spirits and productivity up, it's a small price to pay.

One of the most effective ways to manage your team is to get to know your players as individuals and try to tailor a managerial style that meets their needs. Employees bring all sorts of motivations to the job, and the better you understand them and incorporate them into your leadership approach, the more productive and satisfied your employees will be, and the more successful you and your department will be.

You have an employee who has a strong need for attention and recognition. From the motivational standpoint, the best approach is to help her understand that when she performs successfully on the job, she will get the positive reinforcement she seeks. This is a compelling way to make the work highly motivational for her.

While you may be tired of giving compliments, she obviously never tires of hearing them. And, that probably applies to many of your employees.

To quote the experts

Q. We have a new employee in our professional group who is always citing or quoting some study or person. There is rarely a need for this in most of our discussions. How do we tell him?

A. It is ironically tempting to cite an appropriate response, such as the words of Sydney Smith (1771-1845), "What you don't know would make a great book." However, because this particular employee seems to be most comfortable in the world of citations and quotations, this may not be the way to go.

There is no particular reason why some people feel compelled to communicate in such a way that their comments need footnotes. For some, there may be underlying insecurities, and flashing this knowledge may make them appear and feel more intellectual. Others are in fact highly intellectual, and this is part of the way that their minds work.

Because you are dealing with a new employee, this may merely be part of the way that he copes with new situations. As he becomes more comfortable, there may be fewer citations.

Regardless, rather than being incited by his tendency to cite, it makes more sense for you to focus on his performance, effectiveness, and contributions to your department. It is possible that his arguably eccentric behavior may lead to increased departmental creativity. At the same time, it may be helpful to take a look at yourself and the possibility that this new employee's expertise may be making you feel a little insecure.

Flirting with insecurity

Q. I work in a bank, and some of the other women I work with claim that I flirt with the male customers. I'm friendly to all the customers, and I resent being called a flirt. How can I change this false image of me?

A. The one person who definitely knows if you are flirting is you. Deep down, the flirt always knows. If you are flirting with the customers, it's also worth noting that you are flirting with trouble. But, if you can honestly say that you are not a flirt, that's the end of this issue.

In terms of dealing with the mistaken image of you, there is not much direct action to take. If it makes you feel better, you can approach the gaggle of coworkers and discuss the matter. However, don't expect them to suddenly change their opinions. The problem is that you can look at your behavior and see an animated, personal, and enthusiastic approach to your customers, while the gaggle looks at the exact same behavior and sees an advanced stage of amorous banking.

The reasons for their determination that you are flirting are probably based on some wishful thinking. For example, they may be jealous of your friendly style of dealing with the customers and wish that they could do the same. Because they cannot, they redefine it as flirting. Perhaps they have actually done some flirting in the past, or secretly wish that they could be doing so now, but that's not in the cards. This draws them to the issue of flirting and causes them to see it in cases where it does not exist.

The fact is that the comments about your supposed flirting did not come from your manager, and there obviously has not been a groundswell of complaints from the customers. Just because some fellow employees have gone petty does not mean that you need to change your behavior.

Regardless of your actions, the little group would keep the flirt label pinned on you because of their own baggage. If you are not a flirt, don't focus on their image of you. It's their problem—not yours. If you want to build better work relationships, focus on some of your other coworkers who do not share the flirting fantasy.

Fear of the unknown and known

Q. How do you deal with an employee who has been laid off in two previous jobs and now fears that the next layoff is right around the corner when it is not? I am tired of having him ask me several times a week if he is about to be laid off. How do I get him to stop?

A. When you are dealing with a person who is basically insecure, you can make pronouncements about job security until the cows come home, and he is going to think that the cows have come home to take his job. The fact is that there is no overnight remedy.

The next time he asks you if a layoff is around the corner, give him an honest answer that nothing has changed. Tell him that you are becoming increasingly concerned about his repeated questions in this area, and then ask for his help. Tell him that you do not know what to do to get this behavior to stop, and then ask him to suggest a solution. He may be able to come up with his own commitment to change, and that can be a step in the right direction.

You may also want to suggest that he speak to one of the human resources specialists or an employee assistance specialist to discuss this situation further. The irony is that the more he focuses on being laid off, as opposed to focusing on his work, the more he is increasing his chances of losing this job.

Me first

Q. One of the people I work with makes himself the center of everything that's discussed. He shrugs off what we say, but we are expected to listen as he talks endlessly about himself. How do we change this?

A. Your associate's behavior is typical of people who are best described as "security-challenged." They quickly dance through the motions of listening to others, while viewing every discussion as an invitation to a tale about themselves. No matter what the topic, they are always ready to pounce with, "That reminds me of when I...."

In fact, one of the real tell-tale signs of a card-carrying egocentric is the number of times that "I" and "me" invade their conversations.

Dealing with a fellow employee who fills his speech with self-talk is a straightforward matter. If there are business issues to discuss, then you should discuss them. When "I" and "me" start to make their appearance, all you need to do is show some assertiveness and direct the conversation back to the business issue at hand, or, if the discussion is about to end, you can easily excuse yourself on the basis that you have work to do.

A more basic question is why you feel you are "expected to listen" to his stories. He is a fellow employee at your job level, and you are under no formal obligation to remain riveted as he waxes eloquently about himself. Many people are concerned about being impolite in these situations, but by acting in a businesslike manner, you can end a conversation without ending a working relationship. Frankly, many self-talkers are used to having their stories abridged.

By letting the self-talker ramble on, you are actually sending him a message that you are interested in his tales of glory. In essence, you are rewarding the behavior, so he is even more likely to repeat it.

This means that the best way to change this situation is to change your behavior. If you are thinking about trying to change his, it is important to note that the behavior of the self-talker is a direct reflection of his personality, and it would be easier for you to change planes in mid-air than change that. In fact, if you were to give him some friendly feedback regarding his tendency to turn every conversation into a diatribe about himself, you would soon hear, "That reminds me of when I...."

Resigned to resign

Q. One of the managers who reports to me is doing something that I find to be most annoying: whenever he makes a mistake, he asks if he should submit his resignation. I have told him to stop, but he persists anyhow. How do I get him to stop?

A. This manager's behavior has insecurity stamped all over it. Unfortunately, you cannot change the behavior of an insecure manager by issuing an order. In fact, by telling him to stop asking if he should resign, you may have actually fueled his insecurity because he is unable to follow your directive.

The first action to take is to try to determine if there is anything about your leadership style or developments in the company itself that may be exacerbating his feelings of insecurity. If there are threats of layoffs or impending downsizing, or if your style is one of those "my-way-or-the-highway" approaches, you can expect him to continue to quiver.

Although the era of making grandiose promises to employees about their future with a company has passed, there are some steps that you can take to help this manager feel more secure. For example, because insecurity can be heightened because of a lack of information about what is going on in the company, you should consider having increased communication with him about plans, changes, and developments. Let him know more about the near-term and longer-term goals and the strategies to meet them, and try to give him more of an opportunity to express his ideas and suggestions. The more he knows about what is going on, the more secure he is likely to feel.

In addition, increased communication with this manager will also provide him with more of an opportunity to discuss his work with you, and this should lead to a decrease in mistakes and a further increase in his feelings of security.

At the same time, it will be important for you to continue to monitor his mistakes, particularly in terms of their magnitude, frequency, and the extent to which he is learning from them. Unless he starts to show some improvement, you may want to consider his resignation offer more carefully.

No comment

Q. I was at a holiday lunch with several people in our department, including our manager, when one person in the group made a very insulting comment about my intelligence. Everyone suddenly became quiet, but I let it go. Now I am really upset. Should I have said something to him at the time, and what do I do now?

A. The only person at your holiday lunch who demonstrated a lack of intelligence was the person who insulted you. In fact, by letting it go at the time, you demonstrated a high level of restraint, self-respect, and class. Had you lashed back at this individual, all you would have done is drop to his level.

Because the luncheon is over but his comments are still turning your stomach, you should say something to him. However, you need to know at the outset that a person who is foolish enough to make that kind of a comment is also foolish enough to refuse to listen to others. Nonetheless, if it makes you feel better, you can tell him how you feel about the comment, and ask him how he would feel if he had been on the receiving end.

More importantly, keep the big picture in mind: he made a fool out of himself in front of your manager, and you demonstrated to your manager that you are a quality person. If your manager is sharp, he or she will have already spoken to this employee. After all, if your co-worker acts like this during a holiday luncheon, how does he act on a day-to-day basis? If his behavior persists, he may be a candidate for a permanent holiday.

Chapter 14

We Can't Go on Meetings Like This

Over the past few years, meetings at work have been undergoing a major transition that is continuing right now. More and more companies are replacing many of their traditional meetings with teleconferencing and other online solutions. Although these virtual meetings are not perfect, they do hold out the possibility of eliminating many of the logistics associated with pulling employees out of their offices or cubicles and putting them in one location for a face-to-face encounter.

Of course, that advantage may also be the major disadvantage of these meetings as well. In some situations, there is still no substitute for bringing the troops together for a wide-open discussion.

Either way, people at every level of an organization continue to attend meetings, and many spend more time in meetings than in any other singular activity or inactivity at work. The reasons for holding meetings are endless, and, unfortunately, many meetings seem endless, too.

Meetings offer excellent opportunities to capitalize on the synergy of the group to creatively solve problems, set goals, formulate plans, and generally help an organization run more productively and effectively. At the same time, meetings also offer less endearing opportunities to generate dissatisfaction, frustration, and "groupthink."

There are countless ways that jerks can turn meetings into a mess, ranging from poor timing or venue, all the way to muddled objectives, the wrong participants, and totally inappropriate behaviors. However, rather than being worked in meetings, there are proven strategies to help make meetings work.

Reckless on the safety committee

Q. There are eight of us on a safety committee, and we are supposed to make recommendations to make the worksite safer. One member of the committee, not the chairman, has taken it upon himself to send recommendations to management under the name of the committee, even though the committee never agreed to them. We have all spoken to him about this, but you never know what he is going to do next. What can we do?

A. It is ironic that a safety committee would have a loose cannon. Before he launches any more messages in the committee's name, it is time to do more than talk to him about this. All of you have done this already, and yet the messages fly.

The next step needs to be taken by the chairperson. In a word, he or she needs to sit down with the self-appointed messenger and explain the facts of committee life. In a word, if this employee is planning on remaining on the committee, he cannot be unilaterally drafting up recommendations under the committee's name and sending them to management.

He can certainly write recommendations and submit them to the committee itself, but that is where they must stop until the group has made its decisions. He should clearly understand that his current behavior is disruptive, distracting, and interfering with the mission, performance, and objectives of the committee.

He also needs to understand that if he sends any more of these recommendations to management, the committee will send a recommendation to management that he be removed.

A problem of numbers and a number of problems

Q. At our quarterly meeting, one of my colleagues gave a presentation that included overhead projections. On one of his diagrams, I noticed a computational error that changed the accuracy of his conclusion. When I mentioned this in the meeting, I could see him bristle. Afterwards he accused me of hatcheting his presentation. I don't think I did. Was I out of line?

A. It sounds as though his numbers were out of line, and so was his reaction to your comment. However, this assumes that you pointed out the error in a businesslike fashion and without any obvious or subtle verbal jabs.

The purpose of these meetings is often to analyze past performance in various areas and to review the next period's objectives. If there is an error in the analysis, it would be an even larger mistake to overlook it and let the erroneous numbers serve as the basis for future goals.

These types of meetings are most productive when the information that is presented serves as a basis for an open discussion. For example, even if there was not a computational error, it is possible that the objectives for the next period are too high or too low, and this is the exact kind of issue that can come out in a free-flowing discussion.

You should meet with this colleague to further discuss what happened. Make sure he understands that you would expect others to analyze your presentation just as thoroughly. You know at least one person who is going to do so.

Management by invectives

Q. I asked my manager a question during a meeting, and she said I should know the answer to something as simple as that. I didn't think it was a simple question, and I did not like being put down in front of everyone. I still feel embarrassed and angry. If I go to her, I think she'll give me an even harder time, so how do I deal with this?

A. Some managers operate by the philosophy that there is no such thing as a bad question, while your manager's approach is to make those who ask questions feel bad. There is no excuse for her behavior, as it builds ill will, animosity, and distrust.

If your manager did not believe that your question was appropriate, it is only professional to answer it during the meeting, and then discuss her concerns with you in private afterwards. Even if a question during a meeting is not on target, it can still serve to keep the communication lines open and lead to other important topics.

When questions are stifled during a meeting, a point will ultimately arrive when no questions are asked. Your manager can then assume that everyone is in sync, while communication is actually grinding to a halt.

You will feel better by talking about the incident with some of your fellow employees who were in attendance. In addition, no matter how your manager feels about questions, there's little question that it would be helpful if you and some of your associates were to meet with her as a group to talk about communication and the ways to improve it.

Forgotten but not gone

Q. I was on a committee with people from many departments, and we spent long hours working on ways to improve operations. We wrote a thorough plan that was submitted to management, but that was the last we heard of it. What do you suggest we do?

A. Your company may be interested in improving operations, but based on the way that management handled your committee's findings, they do not sound like smooth operators at all. Unless their objective was to generate dissatisfaction, distress, and distrust, there should have been a response to your committee's work.

You have heard the last of your report only if you let that happen. You and your fellow committee members owe it to yourselves and to your company to find out what really happened to your plan. You need to know if it is still being reviewed, if it was deferred, if it was destroyed, or if it has been reborn as shelf liner. In a word, you are entitled to one of today's most popular buzzwords: closure.

One way to obtain such feedback is to advise the committee's leader of the widespread dissatisfaction on this matter, and ask him or her to set a meeting with management. If this is not feasible, then you should consider a letter from the entire committee to management. The letter should not reflect any of your disappointment or dissatisfaction, but rather should be a request to meet with management to discuss the report. Management's reaction, no matter what it may be, will give you a great deal of insight into the real operations of this company.

The setup and the put-down

Q. I run a small department, and my manager scheduled an 11 a.m. meeting with me and two other department heads. At a few minutes before 11, I arrived at the meeting, but it was already going and the topic was focused on how to improve my department (which is running extremely well). I didn't know this was the topic, and I was incensed that they started without me, but I didn't say anything about it. Do I have a right to be annoyed?

A. You walked into an ambush that sounds like a corporate version of the O.K. Corral. And that's not okay.

You certainly have a right to be annoyed, but being annoyed is not going to solve the problem. You should meet with your manager to discuss what happened.

Tell your manager that you are concerned over the way the meeting went, and you are wondering why the discussion about your department started before you arrived. Unless there is a particularly compelling explanation, let your manager know that this kind of format can generate frustration, dissent, and distrust. You should also mention that meetings typically tend to be more effective if the participants are advised of the key topics in advance. The O.K. Corral did not have a happy ending, and neither do meetings that resemble it.

A real sleeper

Q. We have management meetings in the early afternoon twice a week. They are long, boring, and repetitive, and they provide about 20 minutes worth of content in two hours. My problem is that I am having a very hard time staying awake in them. Do you have any suggestions?

A. Early afternoon meetings have often been regarded as the ultimate cure for insomnia. However, this does not have to be the case.

The first step is to look at your own basic energy level. If you find that you frequently run out of gas in the early afternoon, whether you are at a meeting, your desk, or a ball game, then it's time to focus on your own condition rather than on the condition of the meetings. Issues such as diet, exercise, sleeping patterns, stress, illness, and even job dissatisfaction can be playing a role here.

If you find that your energy level is more than appropriate in most other work and non-work situations, and it is just these meetings that are lulling you into dreamland, there are a number of actions to consider. The best way to stay awake in these meetings is to be an active participant. This can be accomplished in many ways, such as by making a brief presentation, asking questions, responding to questions, or voicing suggestions. By becoming actively involved in the meetings, you are far more likely to stay sharp and alert in them.

Look around at your fellow managers during these meetings. If you see their heads following an erratic downward path that ends with the classical upward jolt, it is safe to assume that they are not being exactly energized by the meetings either. To the extent that this is occurring, you should meet with them to discuss some ways to enliven and streamline these meetings, as well as discuss the possibility of eliminating them or replacing them with teleconferencing. The next step would be to meet with your manager to discuss your suggestions.

For example, if you really have 20 minutes of content in two hours, you could suggest that these meetings be held on a stand-up basis, even if held more regularly. Stand-up meetings cut to the issues, keep the lines of communication open, and allow for more direct involvement by the participants. And, they make sleeping a less attractive option, unless the participants are horses.

Where is everyone?

Q. It is most annoying to be expected to attend regular meetings when some of the people who really need to be there are rarely present. This makes the meetings a total waste of time. I have voiced this concern to management, and they agree with me, but then do nothing about it. Can anything be done?

A. Somewhere in time, your company lost sight of the true objective of these meetings and now seems to hold them just for the sake of holding them.

You have already taken the best step in this matter, namely discussing your concern with management. The fact that management agreed with you and then went right on holding the same arguably useless meetings points to rigid thinking and is akin to management saying, "Yes, we agree that holding these meetings is ridiculous, and it is our unwavering intent to continue to be ridiculous."

If there is a level of management that is higher than the one you approached, a meeting with such a topsider may be worthwhile. However, if you have gone as high as you can go, or if you find that the same thinking prevails even at the most senior levels, then it is important to look at the big picture. In doing so, you will probably find many situations that parallel the thinking associated with these meetings. In short, it does not sound as though you are going to find a meeting of the minds here.

Marching to a different band

Q. I was put on a task force with four other people, and we are supposed to look at benefit programs. There is one person in the group who comes late to the meetings, hardly does any work, and is quick to make snide comments. We spoke with our manager, but he feels this individual is important for the group. How do we get anything done?

A. Because this is an ad hoc group, and all this individual does is add havoc, there are few steps to take. You have already taken the most important one, namely to talk with your manager. He could have used his influence and power to help bring this individual into line. Because he opted not do so, your disruptive associate may feel even further emboldened.

The next step is for the four of you to meet with this problematic associate to explore possible ways to work together. One approach is to ask how he would like to work with you. He may be a creative loner who could be more effective by emailing his inputs to the group. If you let him come up with a way to constructively work with you, he just may be able to do so.

If he continues to be a disruptive force, then you and your associates need to revisit your manager, give him an update, and let him see how the project is suffering. Although your group is studying benefits, there will be no benefit unless he takes some corrective action.

About the scheduling

Q. Our company has several branches, that are between 50 and 100 miles from the corporate office. As branch managers, we waste many hours going to and from the office to attend meetings, sometimes three times a week. I told the corporate staff they need to schedule more of these meetings on one day, but they never do this. How do I get through to them?

A. Your company gives a whole new meaning to the importance of having employees with a great deal of drive. In terms of getting through to the corporate staff, you told them that they need to schedule more of these meetings on one day. However, when you tell people what they need to do, they often react with resistance. Try using a sales approach that tailors your comments to the needs, objectives, and style of these corporate personnel.

For example, if they are financial types, you should make a thorough, detailed presentation that spells out the costs of the current scheduling and the savings associated with your approach. By letting them see that your thinking is similar to their thinking, you are far more likely to influence them.

Be sure to mention the value of various high-tech solutions, such as videoconferencing, audioconferencing, and screensharing.

If the meeting schedule still appears to be better suited for stock car drivers than managers, one near-term option is to try to make the rides more productive, such as by listening to management tapes along the way. However, if the lack of topside responsiveness is typical of the way that branch managers are treated, perhaps it is time to focus more on the direction you are driving your career.

And in closing

Q. At the end of a recent meeting, one of my coworkers blurted out that I have not been very effective in carrying out my responsibilities, so her work has suffered. I was caught totally off guard, and then the meeting ended. I spoke with our manager afterwards, but I don't think I had much of an impact. By the way, the employee later apologized for stabbing me in the back. What should I do now?

A. Just as most sporting events cannot end with a penalty, a meeting should not end with an attack. Whoever was running the meeting should have called an audible and kept the meeting going until the matter was resolved.

Your attacker was very clever. She waited until the end of the meeting, and this allowed her destructive comments to be the final thought that the attendees took with them. She scored all of her points, and you scored none. Although you spoke with your manager afterwards, and this was the right thing to do, you already know that the impact was not great.

At this point, you should keep your guard up, make sure your manager and other coworkers are aware of your effectiveness on the job, and give your manager more specific updates on your work.

By the way, the attacker's apology to you was meaningless. Apologizing for stabbing someone in the back does not make the wound disappear. If your coworker wants to start the healing process, tell her to voice her apology to your manager and to your coworkers who attended the meeting.

Chapter 15

Training in Action Versus Training Inaction

Companies today are spending billions of dollars to train their employees. While some of the motive behind this spending is to demonstrate that they are "cool" companies and truly care about their employees, such expenditures are also accurately regarded as investments in the company's most valuable assets, their people.

Investing in employee training and education is critically important in today's competitive marketplace and rapidly changing world. When companies fall behind in the development of their human resources, it is not surprising to find them falling behind in countless other ways as well. And further, investment in employee development not only strengthens the overall company, it also strengthens individual employee motivation, involvement, and commitment.

At the same time, the area of employee development has not escaped the curse of the jerks. They can be found designing, selling, conducting, implementing, and evaluating programs, as well as insisting on some programs and resisting others. This has led to numerous educational programs that have useless content, simplistic approaches, marginal instructors, canned answers, no practice opportunities, no feedback, and no applicability whatsoever to the job.

And even if the employees are fortunate enough to participate in a highly effective training program, there can be jerks waiting on the job to prevent any new insights or approaches from being implemented.

The fact is that educational programs offer an opportunity to generate a monumental array of problems. Fortunately, these programs also offer an opportunity to generate a monumental array of solutions, particularly for those who know how to separate programs that work from programs with jerks.

Unwarranted claims

Q. We just met with the representatives of a training company, and they seem to have some good programs. One of their most powerful selling points is that turnover dropped significantly in a company where they introduced one of their programs six months ago. How do you view a claim such as this?

A. This type of claim needs to be viewed with a large grain of salt. It is entirely possible that the training company's claim is accurate and their program did contribute to a reduction in turnover. Of course, it is also possible that their training program had nothing to do with it at all.

All that can be said is that the training program was held, and turnover dropped after that. This does not mean that the training program caused the reduction.

Turnover could have dropped as a result of any number of other events occurring simultaneously. For example, the state of the economy can cause people to hold onto their jobs rather than quitting, and turnover can also decrease as a result of new leadership, changes in policies, improved working conditions, and the like.

At this point, the best step is to look carefully at your company's training needs, the specific objectives you want the training program to meet, and the way that the program focuses in these areas.

You should also probe into the techniques the training company plans to use to measure and evaluate the program's effectiveness. If the would-be trainers avoid these questions, you should avoid the trainers.

Anyone for training?

Q. I am a new employee with this company, and I have been given no training. When I have questions about how to do my job, my supervisor ignores me, and my coworkers are too busy. I'm making mistakes already, and I don't know where to turn. Can you help?

A. If you entered this position with the clear understanding that you are going to be provided with some training by your supervisor or colleagues, only to find that such training is nonexistent, then it is quite likely that many other components of effective management are also nonexistent.

Even if you were hired because of your expertise, along with an expectation that you needed minimal training if any, there still is a need for someone in management to meet with you to review the company's standards and mode of operation in your position. By ignoring all of your requests, your supervisor is also ignoring the broad range of present and potential costs associated with an employee who is either minimally productive or making substantial errors.

If you truly want to keep this job, you should approach the supervisor when he or she is not particularly busy and ask for some help. Be clear and concise in describing the specific areas where you need guidance. You can take a similar approach with your fellow employees, and even with human resources or senior management if necessary. You work for a company that wittingly, unwittingly, or half-wittingly expects you to sink or swim on your own, but you should give it a little more time before deciding whether to jump ship.

Short cuts or short-sighted?

Q. I am new here and I just completed the orientation program. Now that I am on the job, the other employees are telling me to forget about most of what I learned in the orientation and use their shortcuts. I feel uncomfortable doing this. What should I do?

A. In some cases, employee shortcuts are actually a better way to do a particular job, while in other cases these shortcuts can short circuit an entire operation.

The real question focuses on your department manager. If he or she is aware of the shortcuts and feels that they are a better way to handle various operations, then they should be documented and included in the orientation.

However, if your manager is aware of the shortcuts and believes they are compromising quality, then one has to question why he or she is allowing them to be used. It is possible that there is a performance bonus involved here, and your manager has decided to look the other way and focus only on output.

And finally, if your manager is unaware of these shortcuts altogether, one has to wonder how this individual is spending his or her time.

Because it is difficult for you to do your job under these circumstances, you should meet with your manager to discuss what is going on here. Your manager's response is going to tell you a great deal about what it means to work in this company, especially if his or her reaction to the shortcuts is to cut you short.

The missing mentor

Q. When I joined this company about a month ago, I was assigned a mentor, but I can never find her. If I do track her down, she is always too busy to help me or even set an appointment. I told my manager about this, and he offered no help. What do you suggest?

A. It is difficult enough to have a mentor who is not mentoring, but when you combine it with a manager who does not seem to be managing, you have a work situation that is hardly workable. However, there are a couple of steps that can help.

Although some people who hold the title of mentor are little more than tormentors, there are usually other people in the workplace who can be highly helpful and supportive, even if they hold no formal title. You should talk to some of your fellow employees and see if any of them can help you during this orientation period. It would not be surprising to find an informal mentor among the group.

If you find that you still cannot get any adequate guidance, then you should consider talking to the human resources representative if there is one, or else take your concerns higher in the organization. The larger problem is the way the new hires are treated can paint a rather clear picture of a company's overall style, standards, and objectives. In your situation, this does not sound like its a very pretty picture.

It's getting difficult

Q. I'm going to a seminar about dealing with difficult people at work, and my manager just told me that he expects me to make a presentation about the seminar to the rest of our group when I return. I don't want to do it. Is it fair for him to make this request?

A. It should not take a seminar on difficult people at work for you to realize that you are behaving like one right now. Your company is spending money for you to attend the seminar and is also paying your salary while you are away. It is not asking too much for you to share what you have learned.

There is growing emphasis today on managing the knowledge that employees bring to work and having employees play a greater role in educating each other. Being expected to educate your coworkers after attending a seminar is part of this trend.

The fact that management selected you to attend this seminar can easily be interpreted as a vote of confidence in you. And further, having a chance to present new information to your fellow employees is a real opportunity to showcase yourself.

You are actually going to learn far more in the seminar because you are going to be doing some training afterwards. You should approach this entire project with positive expectations, and that's just how difficult people should be approached as well.

Pontificating, not educating

Q. Our company has a training consultant who comes here two days a month, and we all think it is worthless. We have to interrupt our work to listen to him pontificate, and it is a waste of time and money. When we express our dissatisfaction to our manager, he says that he likes him. We don't know what to do. What can you suggest?

A. When training does not connect with trainees, it is time to disconnect the program. However, much will depend on your manager's reasons for liking the program. If he thinks it is doing some good, there are ways to bring him up to date. But if he is the trainer's brother-in-law, things do not resolve so easily.

Assuming there is no political or familial reason for your manager to stay with this program, you and some of your fellow employees should discuss the situation with him. Let him know that you appreciate the company's emphasis on training, and you want to make sure that the company is getting its money's worth.

If there are specific components of the program that are inappropriate, out of date, or out of touch, you should discuss each. You should also be ready to suggest some better training programs. If your manager is not swayed, you should suggest something that every truly professional training program contains: an evaluation. When conducted properly, evaluations can provide real documentation regarding the value of a training program.

The next step is obviously up to him. If he is well-trained, he will be highly interested in making sure that you are, too.

Hot topics

Q. There is talk that our company is going to conduct a major team-building program, culminating in having the employees do what is called a "fire walk." I understand this means that we will be walking on hot embers. Could this be true? If it is, several of us don't want any part of it.

A. It sounds as though the proposed team-building program is already working, because several of you have coalesced into a team that opposes the whole thing. As for your question, the answer is, yes, there are some hot programs that indeed finish up with the participants putting their feet to the fire.

There is considerable debate over the value of these programs, whether they have the participants walking on fire, climbing ropes, riding mechanical bulls, or playing with blocks. There is much to be said for experiential learning, and there are widespread credible supporters who contend that these types of programs have a positive permanent impact on employee cohesiveness, growth, and productivity.

At the same time, there are other credible sources who question the value of these programs, contending that there is minimal transference to the job, and the so-called amazing feats, such as fire walking, can be easily explained away.

As for your concern about fire walking per se, there have been countless glowing reports, along with a few indicating that the amazing feat ended up being blistered feet. At this point, you need to talk to management and find out all you can about the program. If it is sprung on you as a surprise, that's not saying much for your company's true commitment to teamwork. And at the end of the day, if you are not fired up about doing a fire walk, pass on it.

Good stuff, but not here

Q. My company sent me to a training program, and when I returned I was going to implement some new techniques about managing different personality types. When I told my manager, he reacted very negatively and said there is no time for any of that. I think I can be more effective if I at least try to apply what I learned. How should I go about doing this?

A. Because you went to a seminar that dealt with personality types at work, you should have applied some of what you learned when you approached your manager. After all, it sounds as if he could score well above average when it comes to being hostile-aggressive, over-controlling, insecure, or rigid.

One of the real problems with many training programs goes back to a buzzword called "transference." A training program may be regarded as excellent by all educational standards, but unless it truly fits into the trainee's organization, the program is doomed to failure. Your manager is a roadblock that is preventing everything you learned from transferring into your job.

However, it does not have to be this way. Part of the problem is that you approached him with a "done deal." A better approach is to meet with him, share your newly-acquired expertise with him, and then discuss the ways that both of you can implement some of the new strategies, at least on a trial basis.

The one caveat behind all of this is that you should be careful about locking personality labels on those around you. People are complex, and by labeling them, you may find that there can be some unflattering labels pasted on you.

Now hear this

Q. My manager just returned from a week-long seminar, and now he is using all sorts of new jargon and contrived speech patterns when communicating with us. It's driving us crazy. Things were not going so badly before, and we don't know what to do now.

A. Your manager literally and figuratively bought the words and wisdom of the seminar leader. He spent a week seeing and hearing the marvels of his newly-acquired communication skills, and now he is ready to apply them in his department. The problem is that the department is not ready for him.

It is most uplifting to attend a seminar and come back with some visible and measurable skills that can be instantly applied to a department. At the same time, although various new technical skills can be plugged in without too much disruption, new interpersonal skills are not as easy to implement. They worked well in the week-long seminar at which everyone was using them, but they can have a Martian-like quality when brought back to one's own department.

If your manager is intent on applying his newly-learned communication skills, the first and ironic step that he needs to take is to communicate with all of you about them. In failing to do so, all he has succeeded in doing is to unilaterally introduce a key change in the department. Your resistance is the normal and typical employee reaction.

Before allowing his new approach to generate further distress for you and your fellow employees, sit down with him and ask for more information about this new communication style. Many organizations actually expect managers who return from seminars to conduct their own mini-seminar within the company in order to bring all of the employees up-to-speed on the newly-acquired knowledge. You should ask him for such a session.

At the same time, presumably you have some degree of understanding of your manager. Is he the kind of person who jumps from one managerial fad to another, only to leave his career path strewn with discarded buzzwords, modalities, and systems over the years? If so, you can sit patiently because this new approach too shall pass. At the same time, if he is a cautious, reflective, and deliberative manager, your career path is about to have some entirely new road signs.

Truth be told

Q. Our manager sends us articles on management. Some are okay, but the most recent one was ridiculous. I know the other supervisors feel the same way about it, but when he asks them, they'll say the article was very helpful. Should I follow their politically-correct ways, or tell him what I really think?

A. Your manager is probably not sending you these articles so that you will learn how to say they are helpful. If you think he's that kind of manager, then you have more to rethink than the article's content.

If he truly believes these articles are important, then that's how you should approach them. If the most recent one seems to make no sense, you should mention that to your manager when he asks for your opinion.

However, this does not mean you should say the article was ridiculous. A better approach is to use questions. For example, you can indicate that a specific point seemed confusing or contradictory, and then ask if he can clarify it. As your manager answers your question, you might see that the article is not so ridiculous. And your manager might see that you are actually thinking about what he has sent you.

Either way, by asking some intelligent questions about the article, you will be sending a message about yourself that is far more compelling than the politically-correct banter of your associates.

Bad timing

Q. Every quarter, we are required to attend a training seminar. For the third year in a row, one of the topics is time management, and it is the same class I attended twice already. When I told my manager we need something new, he said that time management is always worthwhile. Does this sound worthwhile to you?

A. It is ironic that a seminar on time management can be a waste of time. If this is the same course you already had twice, and not a new or more advanced version, then it does not sound particularly worthwhile.

While time management is indeed important, attending the same course three times is pushing the limit. Training programs should not be selected solely on the basis of a general belief that a topic is important. Rather, training should be implemented on the basis of needs. If there are real and measurable problems with time management in the organization, some additional training in this area is warranted.

A truly effective training program also includes specific objectives, cutting-edge training technologies, opportunities for practice and feedback, and an evaluation system to determine if the training has actually met its goals.

The fact that your company is making a commitment to employee growth and development is a very positive sign, but it sounds as though the time has come to review the time management component and the objectives of the overall program itself.

The bottom line

Q. A few months ago, we spent a considerable amount of money on a sales training program, and we know from surveying the attendees that they enjoyed it and learned a lot. The problem is that we are seeing no change in their sales numbers. How do we get such a positive reaction to the program and nothing else?

A. One problem is that your survey focused more on reactions than behaviors. You found that your salespeople enjoyed the program and learned something from it. That's very nice, but that does not mean there has been any change in their sales strategies, practices, or behaviors.

You can go to a great seminar on making soufflés, and a survey might show that you learned something and enjoyed it. However, that does not mean you will be able to whip things into shape when the heat is on and you have a spatula in hand. What you actually need is a survey that measures sales behaviors after the training, and, preferably before the training as well.

At the same time, maybe the situation has nothing to do with the survey. Perhaps the new skills of your sales team have been undercut by other developments, such as increased competition, price wars, new alternative products, or larger changes in the economy. In fact, sales might be far worse if the team had not been trained.

One step to take at this time is for the sales managers to follow-up with the salespeople, directly observe their sales techniques, and then provide some guidance, feedback, and modeling to help them heat things up.

Chapter 16

Dollars, Sense, and Incentives

Not surprisingly, issues related to money and incentives continue to have a major impact on employee satisfaction, turnover, motivation, and productivity. Looking more carefully at the issue of money and motivation, it is important to emphasize that research continues to show that money per se is not motivational. Rather, it has become increasingly clear that the best way for money to have a positive motivational impact is to tie monetary rewards to performance.

This of course means that money can also have a negative motivational impact. This typically occurs when a company has pay practices that are arbitrary, inequitable, or incomprehensible. When employees sense that they are not being rewarded fairly, there is a marked increase in dissatisfaction, resentment, absenteeism, and turnover.

There are still plenty of jerks whose understanding of monetary rewards is strictly nickel and dime, but that has not stopped them from administering pay and incentive programs. These individuals somehow still believe that it is essential to maintain secrets about pay policies and practices, and then base rewards on something other than performance.

These misconceptions can lead to pay practices that provide newer employees more money than the experienced long-termers, raise practices that do little more than raise employees' hackles, useless incentive programs, and hollow financial commitments.

At the same time, there can also be jerks on the receiving end of a company's pay and incentive program. These are the employees who are quick to express dissatisfaction with pay practices and policies that are more than fair. Their comprehension of pay-related matters is somewhere south of clueless. And in a worst-case scenario, when jerks are administering a pay and incentive program for employees who are also jerks, the outcome can only be a staggering monetary mess. Here are some strategies to clean it up.

Pay practices that don't pay off

Q. I work for a large, bureaucratic organization. It is a great company, and the only problem is that the raises are not based on merit. I know of several people who received "needs improvement" on their review and were given 5 percent increases, while others received "meets job requirements" (two rankings better) and received only 3 percent. Why would a company do this?

A. One of the best ways to create dissatisfaction, dissention, and distrust is to have a random pay increase system, but your company does one better: it actually rewards poorer performers and punishes better performers. Dissatisfaction with pay is based less on the absolute dollar amount that an individual is paid, and more on perception of inequitable treatment.

It is very difficult to find an acceptable explanation for this type of system. It is possible that the merit ratings are only part of the raise system, and other factors such as tenure or performance on key projects are entered into the equation. However, even if there is a decent explanation for your company's practices, the larger problem is that there is far too much secrecy, confusion, and ambiguity surrounding the raise process itself.

Unfortunately, the more likely explanation is that in this large bureaucratic organization, the pay increase policies have evolved into a confusing, cumbersome, clunky mess, with different managers applying different standards and subsequently inconsistent increases.

Cleaning up the pay increase policy is probably on someone's list of things to do. Perhaps a discussion with your manager or the Human

Resources Director will help get this policy out of the "needs improvement" category.

What do employees really want?

Q. Our manager told us that he heard that employees today seek recognition more than anything else at work, including money. He said that we need to keep this in mind when supervising in our areas. I think this is an oversimplification, but when I said this to him, he said I was flat-out wrong. Am I?

A. A manager who tells his employee that he is flat-out wrong is usually flat-out wrong. A more productive managerial response is to discuss your points.

However, if you simply said to him that his thoughts are an oversimplification, your comments may have been perceived as an attack. If you disagree with your manager on this type of issue, you can increase the likelihood of a discussion rather than a brush-off by starting with a question rather than an answer.

As for your manager's thoughts about recognition, he is correct, but only to a point. Recognition is motivational at work, providing that other basic work elements are perceived as fair and adequate, such as the pay, working conditions, and benefits. For example, if the pay is perceived as inequitable, all the recognition in the world is not going to have much of a motivational impact.

However, once the basic elements such as pay are taken care of, then recognition can play an important motivational role, as can advancement, responsibility, achievement, and the work itself. Your manager needs to recognize that there is more to motivation than recognition.

Let's talk cash

Q. Our company has a policy that says we are not supposed to talk about our pay, but everyone does anyhow. I don't see the point of this policy, and I'm wondering how common it is.

A. It's ironic that money talks, but employees are not supposed to talk money. However, employees do talk money, and when there is a policy of secrecy on this subject, all that really happens is that their conversations are filled with inaccuracies.

Policies in this area are premised upon various archaic notions. One is that employees don't know enough about pay to talk about it, and the other is that if employees are allowed to talk about money, the topic will consume them. Of course, none of this could be further from the truth. There are some companies that take a different tack and cling to a policy of pay secrecy simply because it is a tradition.

The truth is that growing numbers of companies are becoming far more open regarding their policies in this area. Some are even taking extra steps to make sure that employees fully understand the pay systems and levels.

Companies that have equitable pay systems are typically comfortable in letting the employees see how they work, and doing so also lets the employees know that management regards them as adults. And further, studies are now finding that there are increases in pay-related satisfaction when employees can openly talk about pay.

The bottom line is that growing numbers of companies are finding that it pays to let employees talk about pay.

A little consistency here

Q. Throughout last year, our company was in a cost-cutting mode, and we all worked extremely hard to make our numbers. That's why we were shocked by the extravagance of the year-end party. As a manager, how do I keep my employees focused on cost reduction after the company does something such as this?

A. It can be hard to maintain the company's party line on cost cutting when the company party ignores the bottom line altogether. At the same time, when a company gives a party that seems to be an inappropriate ending to the story that has been told during the year, it is best to remember that companies have these types of events for all sorts of reasons, from the sublime to the ridiculous.

For example, some topsiders regard this type of party as a way to provide the employees with a major thank-you for their hard work during the year. In other cases, management views this type of party as a tradition, and there is concern as to what the employees would think if it were scaled down.

The best step is for you to have a clear understanding of the rationale behind your company's party, and for you to communicate it to your employees. You can certainly add your opinion, and even indicate that you will check into the possibility of having more employee inputs and involvement in planning any such event for the coming year.

Having taken this step, the party is history. Your employees now need to focus on the future, or they can run the risk of being history, too.

Raising the bar or the barriers

Q. Last quarter, I beat my sales quota by more than 100 percent. Now my sales manager has raised my quota to a number that is just about impossible to reach. This is not fair, and I want to know if there is a way to get him to change it back.

A. You report to a sales manager, but his understanding of sales and management sounds a little thin. When a salesperson roars past his or her established quota, a more appropriate managerial response is congratulations, support, and recognition. Your manager's response is actually a punishment, and it sends a clear message to the rest of the troops: Don't be too successful.

One approach is to treat your manager as a customer and try to sell him on a more appropriate quota. When you meet with him, be sure to use questions and statements that generate many yes responses, and listen carefully to what he says. Once you get a clear understanding of his needs, try to show him how the original quota system will meet these needs more effectively than the new quota. As part of your presentation, include words that have a strong positive emotional charge for him, such as "profit," "growth," and "success."

The fact is that challenging goals have been consistently found to be motivational, while overly demanding goals undercut drive and performance. When sales managers push quotas through the roof, they often push salespeople out the door.

Two is not better than one

Q. I work for a large company and my duties are split between two separate departments. In going over my paycheck, I am certain that I am being paid more than I am supposed to be. I mentioned this to a few friends, and they told me to forget about it because it's the company's problem, not mine. I'm not sure I agree. What do you think?

A. The confusion over your pay system is indeed the company's problem, but the confusion over ethical behavior is your problem. The fact is that you are being paid more than the agreed-upon amount for your position, and you are taking funds that you have not earned and do not deserve.

There are undoubtedly many people who would simply turn their backs on this situation and pocket the money until the company figures it out. However, something deep inside you is telling you that doing so is wrong. That is why you discussed it with your friends, and that is also why you ignored their advice. Your conscience is saying that this is wrong, no matter how your friends try to rationalize it.

If you are still confused about what to do, think about which decision would you feel more comfortable explaining to your parents, your children, or your clergyman or clergywoman? Which decision would you prefer to see on the front page of the newspaper?

Don't forget that when people do good, they often do well. When you tell the appropriate personnel that you are being overpaid, your image in the company is going to be greatly enhanced, and that can be far more profitable than a payroll error.

A disincentive program

Q. Our company gives incentives and awards to employees in other departments, but ours is overlooked. We talked to our manager about this, and he said there is nothing he can do because our work is not set up this way. What should we do?

A. Your manager may indeed lack the power to do anything about these incentives for you and your fellow employees, or he may lack the initiative or skills to do so.

There are ways for companies to provide employees in any job with opportunities to earn incentives and awards. Whether on an individual, group, departmental, or company-wide basis, each employee can participate in some sort of reward program.

Depending on your responsibilities, there can be an array of incentives associated with quality, service, productivity, attendance, work beyond the call of duty, and any other number of positive behaviors. You should do some homework and put together some suggestions as to the best way to set up such a program in your department.

Your next step is to meet with your manager again and show him your ideas. Be sure to ask for his inputs, and then indicate that you want him to take the proposal to senior management. If he still says there is nothing he can do, believe him. Take the proposal to management yourself.

As a side note, some companies provide cash bonuses to their employees based on the usefulness of their suggestions. There are several reasons for you to suggest such a system in your proposal.

A little perspective

Q. Our small company is in a financial squeeze, and none of us got a raise last year. Two employees have been called up in the Reserves, and management announced that the company will be making up the difference between their military pay and regular pay. I don't want to sound as if I am an ingrate, but it doesn't seem right to give them pay for doing nothing here. Besides, we will have to do extra work while they are gone.

A. Your fellow employees are not going on a tour of the Greek isles, but rather a tour of military duty where they may be called upon to put their lives on the line. It's true that you may be doing some extra work while they are overseas, but stop and think about the extra work they are doing for you.

Under the Uniformed Services Employment and Reemployment Rights Act, employers are basically required to excuse employees for military service and then to reinstate them in the position with the rights and benefits they would have had if they had not been called away for duty.

Employers can do more if they wish, such as continuing a portion of the Reservists' pay or covering the cost of continuing their benefits. Employers who exceed the basics of the act may find increases in loyalty, good will, and even publicity, but most take these extra steps out of a sense of what is right.

You are fortunate to work for an employer who goes to bat for the employees. You are also fortunate to work with Reservists who go to bat and battle for you.

Payback time

Q. I go to lunch a few times a week with my boss, and he usually asks me to pay for him. Sometimes he pays me back, but he usually doesn't. Because he's my boss, I'm reluctant to ask him for the money. What can I do?

A. One way or another, your boss needs to understand that there is no such thing as a free lunch. If your boss is intentionally failing to pay you back for the lunches, he is basically a bully.

At the same time, if he is unintentionally failing to repay you, that can be a different story. For example, he might be one of these global thinking visionaries for whom lunch money is inconsequential. Or, on a less favorable note, perhaps he is simply too self-absorbed. Either way, unless you take action, you are going to continue to feed him, and he is going to continue to feed you a line.

There are several ways to deal with this. The most obvious is to avoid going to lunch with him, or else doing so with others. At least in the latter case, you can spread the costs among the group. You can also go to lunch with him and have only enough cash to pay for yourself, assuming the restaurant does not take credit cards. Besides, if it does, why can't it take his?

The final strategy is to catch him in an upbeat mood, tell him you need his advice, and then describe the current situation. His response will give you some real food for thought.

This is no prize

Q. Our company put on a little contest and I won. The prize was not a big deal, but I never got it. When I went to the manager, he said he'd get around to it, but he never has. I don't want to make an issue out of this, but I'm really upset. What do you suggest I do?

A. When companies put on a little contest, only to ignore the little rules, it is a sign of management with little skills. The larger question in your situation is whether this type of behavior is extremely rare, or it is yet another example of management's belief that commitments also mean little.

If the delay in presenting you with your prize is an aberration, you can certainly go back to your manager and mention that you are suffering from prize deprivation and just want your reward. Be sure to pick a time when he is not extremely busy.

However, if it is typical of your manager to conveniently forget about your prize, you can still approach him and tell him that you would appreciate getting the prize, express your concern over what happened, and then ask him what he would do if he were in your situation. Then follow his advice. You always have the option of approaching his manager, but the real question is whether this issue is worth it.

Many companies have found that contests can be a great source of improved satisfaction, motivation, and even productivity. However, if handled with the least bit of inequity, they can be a greater source of distrust, distress, and dissatisfaction. And this latter outcome is virtually guaranteed when the manager is no prize.

Rework these rewards

Q. The company for which I work has a program to reward us for giving good customer service. The problem is that the reward means the employee is placed in a drawing for some prizes. I have been singled out for excellent customer service several times, and I get into the drawing, but I have never won a prize. What do you think of this kind of program?

A. This program sounds like a football game where players who score a touchdown are put into a drawing to see if they get six points. Players who reach the end zone are not going to be satisfied or motivated when they are told to keep up the good work and maybe next time they'll get on the scoreboard.

For incentive programs to be truly motivational, there needs to be a meaningful reward attached to the desired behaviors. Providing employees with the possibility of receiving a prize is not going to cut it, especially over the long term.

If your company is intent on using some kind of drawing, there are a couple of changes that could easily upgrade the program. In the first place, all employees who qualify for the drawing should be given formal recognition, including notation of their stellar performance in their file. In addition, employees who qualify for the drawing more than a given number of times should either be given a prize automatically, or have improved odds with each successive drawing.

A motivational program that is perceived as arbitrary, unfair, or poorly structured is better described as a demotivational program.

Indifferent to the differential

Q. I was recently promoted to a managerial position, but I am disappointed with the salary increase. The average salary for someone in my position is $16,000 more. I met with my boss and argued for an increase, and he said that he will think about it. It has been a month and I still haven't heard anything. Rumor has it he ignores these types of requests for as long as possible. Any suggestions?

A. If you were to go to a sales meeting, would you get into an argument with the customer to convince him or her to buy your product? Probably not.

When you are asking for a pay increase, think of it as a sales meeting. Start by picking the right time. Avoid periods when your manager is busy or upset, and look for periods when you have been particularly successful.

During these meetings, be sure to make many comments that will generate agreement from him. The more he agrees with what you are saying, the more likely he is to say yes later in the discussion. Try to use words that have a strong positive emotional charge for him, such as "profit," "achievement," "success," and "excellence."

You can certainly bring in some salary comparisons, but you should also have an idea of the value that you add. Take a look at your skills, education, experience, and performance and let your manager see the clear contribution that you are making well in excess of your current salary.

As for the delay of a month and the rumor that your manager ignores these requests, the best step is to keep following up. After all, asking for a raise calls for sales skills, and successful selling calls for persistence.

Chapter 17

All in the Family Business

It is now estimated that there are at least 17 million family businesses scattered across the United States, and they range literally from mom-and-pop operations to Fortune 500 Corporations. The most common problem that virtually all of them faced in the past and many still face today is premised upon whether they are a family *business* or a *family* business.

Those that truly operate as a business have a far greater chance of success than those that operate as a family. By functioning as a business entity rather than a family gathering, decisions can be made on a professional, rational, equitable, and businesslike basis for all of the employees.

Those that operate primarily as an extension of the family tend to face a constant parade of family problems along with untold rounds of conflict, complaints, chaos, and crises. Decisions about hiring, firing, transfers, promotions, and assignments are all tougher in these entities because there are emotionally-charged family considerations that cloud business judgment and considerations at every step along the way.

Also in the *family* business, there is the issue of role conflicts. For example, although the owner's son is supposed to be a vice president, the owner/father may still treat him as his baby boy. This can lead to the use of kid gloves and undue favorable treatment. And when the rest of the employees tire of the baby, the babying, and the babysitting, their reactions tend to be a combination of dissatisfaction, resentment, and frustration. These are not the best building blocks for organizational growth and success.

While almost every family has its proverbial jerks, there is no need for them to populate the family business. But when the time comes to hire junior, promote the son-in-law, or let the spouse start changing things around, many family businesses start to show their true colors.

The problems that family-based decisions can create for a business are serious business. As is spelled out in more detail below, the best solution for these problems is a businesslike solution.

That Son of a Boss

Q. I work in the corporate office of a family business, and the president's teenage son was just hired to help us out during the summer. He is a spoiled and inconsiderate person who keeps his own hours, makes endless personal calls, and boasts that he does not have to work at all. We don't want to insult the president, but we are already at our wits ends. What should we do?

A. Although the president's son was hired to help you out, it is obvious that you want to help him out—preferably out the door.

Because that is not a feasible option, your first step is to speak directly with him. If you have not done so already, there should be some introductions, explanations of everyone's roles, clarification of expectations, and a chance for him to talk. You could even do this over lunch. If he gets to know you and your associates more as individuals and less as objects who work for his Daddy, he may be more respectful of you, your jobs, and his job.

If you find that he cannot get out of his brat mode, then you should speak to your department manager about him. Most managers do not take kindly to employees who generate dissatisfaction, unrest, and disruption, regardless of their family ties. Your manager is literally and figuratively in a better position to talk to this employee as well as to his father if necessary. It's always good to know if a family business focuses more on family or business, and you are about to find out.

In's and out's with in-laws

Q. I hired my brother-in-law for a management position not long ago, and it's already apparent that he is failing. However, I have real concerns about the impact on our family if I terminate him. What do you suggest?

A. The most important thing to keep in mind is that there is a real difference between a family tree and an organization chart. The more that you let the former influence the corporate ladder, the less effective you and your company will be.

If any employee is sinking on the job, you need to respond in a business-like way. This means that the first step is to sit down with your brother-in-law, review his performance, and see if there is anything that you can do in terms of increased guidance, training, follow-up, or support. He needs to know precisely how he is doing, and the two of you should jointly develop specific plans and objectives to correct any problem areas. It is important for your brother-in-law to understand the upside potential associated with improved performance, along with the consequences associated with continued marginal work.

As uncomfortable as it is to deal with a relative whose performance is not up to par, it is important to remember he is probably feeling doubly bad not only because of the failure, but because he is failing in your eyes. The family matter weighs heavily on him and he is probably sensing high levels of stress and embarrassment. In fact, he is probably more concerned than you are about the impact of his performance on the family.

As is a good idea with any employee, it makes sense to see if there is a more appropriate position for him within the company. Perhaps he will be more squarely pegged in another hole.

However, if there is nothing available, and you have given him every fair and agreed-upon opportunity to succeed, he can be terminated...but not exterminated. This means that you do not just show him the door. Rather, the most equitable and constructive method is to use an outplacement approach where he is given guidance and support in understanding his own strengths and skills and in locating a more suitable position. As for the family reaction, they will probably be relieved that he has been relieved.

Oh, brother

Q. My older brother runs our family business, and I report to him. We are very different personalities. He is very detail-minded, and I am more of a free spirit. The problem is that he treats me as if I were a child. How do I get him to change?

A. Regardless of personality differences, there are often difficulties reporting to big brother. After all, he spent years being bigger, stronger, and wiser than you, and it may be hard for him to recognize that you have grown up.

However, one important question is whether you actually have grown up. By describing yourself as a free spirit, you may be saying that you are not totally in step with things such as corporate demands, commitments, and responsibilities, as spontaneity is the hallmark of your life. Before looking at your brother's behavior, you need to take an honest look at yours.

The issue is whether your free-spirited attitude is a help or hindrance in terms of the operations and success of the company. If you are in a tightly defined position that calls for structured thinking, you may be having some difficulties getting your work done. To the extent that this is occurring, your brother's treatment may be more a reflection of your job performance than his sibling performance.

As the corporate free spirit, you are probably best suited for a job that provides you with autonomy, performance-based rewards, variety, and a good deal of people contact. While this is not an ironclad rule, it makes more sense to have a free spirited sales and marketing department than a free spirited accounting department.

Assuming your performance is up-to-par, keep in mind that you are not going to change your brother, although it is possible to change his behavior. The best step is to meet with him and show him specific examples of situations where he treated you like a child. Indicate that you certainly do not want favorable treatment because of your brotherly relationship, but unfavorable treatment is not acceptable either. Give him some specific suggestions regarding more businesslike actions that he could have taken, and show him why it would make good business sense for him to do so in the future. For a family business to succeed, all of the players need to focus on business rather than family.

Off the chart

Q. The company owner's wife works here in an ill-defined managerial position. She is not trained as a manager, but is a big know-it-all who tells everyone what to do. How do we deal with her?

A. The best way to deal with her is from afar. Many companies have employees who seem to function as little more than walking mines. You don't want to step on one, and you can get hurt even if you go near them. As long as you are not reporting to this person, try to have minimal contact with her.

Unfortunately, sometimes people in her position have a heat-seeking system that brings them into the departments. When this occurs, the best approach is to deal with her in a friendly, professional, and businesslike manner. If she has a self-serving barrage of questions and answers, refer her to your manager.

The biggest mistake is thinking you can win an argument with her. Putting aside the fact that she is the owner's wife, it is all but impossible to prevail with any know-it-all. Bona fide know-it-all's will never concede that you are right, and they can drag out a disagreement with more tenacity than a 200 pound marlin. Even if you score every single point in the debate, you will never see her wave the surrender flag.

If, by some miracle, you do prevail, one major outcome is that you will have succeeded in brow-beating the owner's wife. You may want to think twice about what you are really winning here.

If she is disruptive to your department, you, and your fellow employees should consider two possible approaches. The first is to meet with your manager and point out the specific ways that individual and departmental performance has suffered as a result of her intervention, and ask your manager to help deal with her. At the very least, your manager needs to agree to be the key person in your department to have contact with her.

The second approach is to take a careful look at the owner. Is he the type of person that can be approached on a matter such as this, or is such a meeting nothing but a short-cut to the exit ramp? If he is approachable, the focus should not be a tactical strike against his wife—instead, focus on what is best for her and the company.

The name game

Q. One of the employees who report to me is personal friends with the owner of the company and some of his family. My employee brings out this connection at least once a week, and I think she's doing it so that I won't discipline her or ever think of replacing her. How should I handle this?

A. Your employee is playing a power game, and she is using her personal connections as a wild card to make her organizationally invincible. If she senses that you will overlook her work-related problems, errors, or shortcomings because of her powerful ties, she is going to take advantage of you and continue to raise the stakes.

This employee should be managed in the exact same way that you would manage anyone else. She should not be given favorable treatment in the hope that she will carry back positive messages to the owner, nor should she be singled out for disciplinary action to over-illustrate your desire to be fair.

If she is doing well, she should be given appropriate credit and recognition, and if she is performing poorly, she should be given appropriate coaching and documentation. If you find that providing her with constructive work-related feedback somehow generates problems for you from the owner, then you will have gathered a very valuable piece of insight about this company. The action you then take will give you a valuable piece of insight about yourself.

Now hire this

Q. I work in a family-owned business, and the president wants me to hire his niece to work in our marketing department. She is unqualified, and I don't want to hire her. What should I do?

A. When you work in a family business that is starting to sound like a family reunion, the best step is to meet with the president. However, you should do so only if you are absolutely certain that placing his niece in the job is a major mistake. You need to have a complete understanding of her expertise, or lack of it, along with a clear idea of the demands of the position where she is to be placed.

Your discussion with the owner should focus on the difficulties that arise when a person is placed in the wrong job. Specifically describe the problems and costs that can accrue to the company because of this mismatch, and then specifically describe the kinds of problems that this mismatch will cause for his niece.

If this is the wrong job for her, it will generate stress, dissatisfaction, failure, and embarrassment, and that will just be on the first day. In a word, it is unfair to do this to her.

You should then make some suggestions that may help his niece, such as a better position for her elsewhere in the company, some classes for her to take, or a more suitable line of work. Let the owner see that you are interested in what is best for her and the company. If he still insists that you hire her, you will have learned something important about your own relationship with him.

Slightly different rules

Q. I work in the same department as the owner's son-in-law. He always comes in late, leaves early, and gets very little done. If I worked the way he does, I'd be fired. Is there anything I can do?

A. Unless you have some kind of plan to marry into this family, your options are rather limited. Nonetheless, you should try to figure out what is really bothering you here. For example, if this son-in-law has no impact on your work, but his mere presence annoys you because of what he symbolizes, the problem is yours. It will be far more productive for you to focus on getting your job done. By focusing on him, you are letting him interfere with your work.

After all, if the owner spent a tremendous amount of money on a statue and placed it in your department, you might think that it is a big waste, but you do not have to look at it. And, the more you do, the more annoyed you will become. In your present situation, the owner has put a different kind expensive statue in your department, because this one comes in late and leaves early. In a word, if the son-in-law has as little to do with your work as a statue, that is how he should be viewed.

However, if his work or lack of it is interfering with yours, the first thing to do is meet with him. Tell him that you need his help, and then show him what he needs to do and when he needs to do it.

If he is as responsive as a statue, you should then approach your supervisor. Be sure to pay careful attention, because his or her reaction will give you a glimpse into the future.

Time out for junior

Q. A few months ago, the owner's son was placed in my department. His performance in the beginning was satisfactory, but it has taken a nosedive lately. I want to discipline him, although I am somewhat hesitant because of his family connection. Do you have any suggestions?

A. Just because this is a family business does not mean that you have to put up with monkey business from the owner's son. You should treat Junior as any other employee, and if you are going to discipline him, make sure that you are applying the same standards that apply to everyone.

It sounds as though you are afraid of the owner's reaction as a result of this discipline. If he somehow sides with Junior on this matter, he has clearly decided to run this operation as something other than a business. This type of a reaction not only weakens the character and skills of Junior, but it also weakens the character of the company in many important respects.

At this point, your job is to run your department as effectively and productively as possible. If you allow Junior to play the family card and get away with all sorts of nonsense, it is just a matter of time before the rest of your troops start to resent him and you.

In a word, Junior needs to be disciplined. If Junior's dad gives you a bad time, then this is a good time to look carefully at where the company is going and determine whether you want to go there with it.

Reverse favoritism

Q. I work in a family business owned by my cousin. He is so concerned about avoiding favoritism that he basically avoids me. Whenever I try to discuss work situations or make a suggestion, he says he cannot get involved because I am family. How can I get him to listen?

A. Your cousin is correct in trying to run the family business as a business and not as a family. However, if that is truly his goal, he needs to listen to his employees, whether they are family or not.

This means that your next step is to meet with him. Prior to such a meeting, try to identify some specific situations where it would have made more business sense for your suggestions to be implemented. When you meet with your cousin, show him some specific ways that he and the company would have profited by listening to you.

He needs to understand that your objective is the same as his: to focus on business and not family. When he overlooks you, he is actually making a business decision based on family considerations. That is not fair to him, to you, or to the business.

Be sure to ask for his thoughts on how to deal with this matter. He may have some specific ideas, or he may say that he will try to be more responsive in the future. Either way, if you look at what he does in the future, you will know if there is a future for you.

Chapter 18

Jerks Online

Through the years, the technological advances that have hit the business marketplace at an exponential rate have opened an entirely new arena for jerks at work to practice their wares. In fact, misuse of new technologies has emerged as one of the most rapidly growing areas where problematic workplace behaviors are now found.

With the advent of the Internet, numerous jerks at work have discovered an outlet that fulfills three counterproductive functions easily and quickly. In the first place, the Internet provides them with a way to waste a huge amount of time. There are countless sites for them to visit, none of which has anything to do with work. The more time they spend on sites to check out sports, wedding registries, or porn, the less work they get done.

But there's more. These Internet visits can also be the source of information and images that can be degrading, offensive, disgusting, and hate-filled. That does not stop some employees from leaving them on their screens or even forwarding them to their coworkers. The minimal result is even more wasted time, while the offended viewers or recipients of the virtual garbage may start thinking about making a claim against the company.

And let's not forget the huge amount of time that is wasted by endless e-mail communication, especially arguments and long e-mail messages that are carbon copied to far too many people. The total destruction of basic rules of grammar and syntax is yet another victim of this technological advance, and this renders many messages confusing, ambiguous, and even incomprehensible. And yet another related way to burn up even more time is through useless and inane Instant Messages, many of which are nothing more than instant interruptions.

If this is not enough, online jerks can also wreak major havoc upon a company's computer systems by downloading attachments that include highly malicious viruses. Many companies are introducing strong policies to deal with and prevent these problems. They certainly help, but there continue to be many individuals whose online behaviors continue to be totally out of line.

While technological advances are to be embraced, there is no reason to embrace the jerks that abuse them. For those individuals, there are specific actions that can help redirect or delete some of their ridiculous behaviors.

War of the words

Q. One of my coworkers does most of his communicating by e-mail, and he can be very antagonistic online. In today's e-mail, he basically accused me of being incompetent, and he copied my boss on the note. I sent him a fairly harsh note in return, and the battle went on until I just stopped. How do you deal with someone such as this?

A. There are a few good ways to deal with this type of person, and doing so by e-mail is not one of them. E-mail is great for communicating facts, figures, data, and straightforward information. When e-mail is used for personal matters or disagreements, you are asking for more trouble.

When you see e-mail communications morphing from an exchange of data to an exchange of insults, it is time to select another medium. If your antagonist is within walking distance, and it's amazing how many times this is the case, then you should head over to his office for a little discussion. It is guaranteed to be more productive than an online outburst.

If your coworker is not within walking distance, then you should pick up the phone and give him a call. Although this is not as effective as a face-to-face encounter, it is still closer to real communication than rashly written online words.

When your combative associate realizes that his online assaults are not going to win battles or friends, he is likely to become less interested in dragging you into his virtual war zone.

Virtual venom

Q. When one particular senior manager in this company gets upset, he uses a lot of profanity in his e-mail. Several of us are offended and upset by this, but we are not sure what to do about it. After all, he is in senior management. He does not use this language in person. How do we get the profanity to stop?

A. It sounds as though you are dealing with a classical virtual bully. He's a tough guy when he is online, but not in person. The computer shields him from the responsibility that accompanies real interaction with another human.

The first step is to approach the bully himself, and do so face-to-face. Let him know that his profanity is offensive, hurtful, and demeaning, and you want it to stop in all future communication with you.

If you continue to be targeted by his profanities, go to his manager. Let the manager know that these messages are creating a hostile environment where it is increasingly difficult for you and some of your associates to work. Bring a few examples of the e-mail messages with you. This paper trail can induce senior management to become more proactive in this area.

You can also suggest that management review its e-mail policy and make sure that inappropriate messages, such as those that contain profanity, are clearly prohibited. The virtual bully should be encouraged to keep the following in mind: what would his family think about his messages, and what would a jury think about them?

A possible cover-up

Q. I oversee a department with 11 people, and they all have computers at their desks. One employee wants a cover for his screen so that it can only be viewed by someone who sits directly in front of it, while people who sit at an angle to the screen cannot see anything on it. There is no business need for him to have this filter, and I have had some recent doubts about what he may be doing online. What do you think of his request?

A. When you have doubts about what your employee may be doing online, there is no doubt that you need to act immediately, whether your employee requests a cover or not. There are several ways to find out what employees are doing online, ranging from simply spending more time with them to obtaining equipment that actually displays what your employees have on their monitors.

As for the screen cover, it does sound somewhat suspicious that your employee would request this item out of the blue. However, if his job includes handling sensitive information, there may be a legitimate business reason for the request. In addition, some of these covers reduce glare, and his request may be as simple as that.

If you want to shed more light on this problem, you should meet with this employee to discuss his reasons for this request. Before agreeing to a filter for his monitor, it sounds as though you should monitor his work more carefully.

On vacation and online

Q. When I was on vacation, my boss called me every day with questions, and I spent at least an additional hour a day on e-mail. Now that I am back, I feel as though I had no vacation at all. Is this what vacations have become?

A. For a vacation to provide real relaxation and rejuvenation, it needs to be more than telecommuting from a resort. There are important psychological benefits associated with a vacation, and you receive none of them when you wake up and face questions from your boss and a long line of email messages. The only long line on your vacation should be attached to your fishing pole.

In the future, if you want to get real value for your vacation dollars, you need to make sure that all of your associates understand that you do not wish to be disturbed. Obviously, if there is an emergency or a crisis that requires your attention, you can certainly be called.

You also need to use your own reasonable business judgment in these types of situations. Some positions and jobs are quite difficult to escape, and you might not be able to enjoy your vacation if you are not kept in the loop. Or, if you are immersed in a major project that should have closed weeks before but now extends into your vacation, then communication associated with it is likely to extend into your vacation, too.

When feasible, the best way to have a vacation that can literally and figuratively take you to new heights is to turn off the office.

It seemed funny at the time

Q. I sent a harmless joke on our company e-mail to some of the people who work with me, and several responded by saying how much they liked it. My supervisor's reaction was the exact opposite. She called me in and wrote up a formal reprimand, and then she said that this is a final warning. This sounds unfair to me. What do you think?

A. Did you hear the one about the company that got sued because employees were sending so-called jokes through the e-mail? The less-than-funny fact is that using the company's e-mail for jokes is not a joking matter. You were lucky, as many companies today will terminate an employee for misusing the company's e-mail system.

The problem is that what is funny to one person may be offensive to another, and if that seemingly offensive material travels through a company's e-mail, then the offended person may move into a litigious mode and target the company itself. No matter what the outcome may be, the whole process can be very costly.

At the same time, the fact that you were unaware of your company's policy in this area indicates that your employer needs to take additional steps to publicize it. This is a point you should mention to your manager.

The entire area of humor at work is growing, with more companies placing increased emphasis on the lighter side of work. This has opened the door to a friendlier and more upbeat work atmosphere in many organizations. At the same time, it is important to note that jokes traveling through the company's e-mail system can have costly punch lines.

Junk mail via e-mail

Q. One of my coworkers e-mails me far too many jokes and stories every day, to the point that some days I receive 10 or more from her. I know she means well, but I would like her to stop. How do I tell her without hurting her feelings?

A. It seems that everyone these days is targeted by at least one well-meaning person who feels compelled to forward old jokes, sappy stories, stale parables, useless lists, and urban legends that are packaged as truth. Of course, the easiest way to deal with this is simply to hit the delete button. No fuss, no muss, no hurt feelings.

If you want to get to the source and stop the flow before it starts, there is a fairly easy way to do so at work. Most companies have clear policies stating that the use of company equipment and resources is exclusively for company business, and that includes e-mail. Simply tell this dispenser of e-junk that she putting both of you in violation of company policy and it would be best if she stayed away from the forward button.

Because you have been getting tons of her messages, hopefully she will get this one from you.

Due it rite, witch is moor then spell-check

Q. I have an employee whose job includes writing brief reports. He knows how to write, but his work typically has grammatical errors and words used incorrectly. When I ask him about this, he says he thought the computer would correct it, but it doesn't. How do I get him to make more of an effort to write better?

A. Your employee thought the computer would correct his errors, but many computer programs are knot able to sea miss takes associated with the wrong word. Some programs might put a cute wiggly line under a misused word, but the suggestions to correct it might not be of much help. The software program for this computer did not even use one wiggly line in spite of the mistakes in this paragraph.

It will be helpful to do more than ask your employee about the problem. He needs to understand that the written assignments he submits to you must be correct, and that means more than passing over the low hurdles posed by a computer's spelling and grammar check. He needs to reread his work carefully and then give it to you.

If he will not do this, then you are dealing with insubordination. And if he cannot do this, then the two of you should sit down and jointly formulate a plan to help him build his writing skills. There are many books and courses that can help.

His response is going to show you where he stands on this matter, and you are then either going to see an employee in action or an employee's inaction.

The write thing

Q. Several of the employees who report to me communicate horribly in writing. There are errors of punctuation, capitalization, and grammar throughout their written communications. The problem is not just in e-mail, but it appears in the formal letters that they send to customers and management. They say I am "old school" because I am concerned about this, and they add that they get their messages across to others, and that is what's important. I disagree on all counts. What about you?

A. Your employees can claim that you are "old school" on this matter, but the truth is that they should return to their "old school" and learn how to write correctly.

Starting sentences without capital letters and totally misusing or forgetting about commas, apostrophes, and periods may be passable when one is sending extremely basic data. However, when there is something of substance to be communicated, messages can be confusing, inaccurate, or muddled in some other way if the sender has a marginal ability to write properly.

For example, someone may write, "I saw your side of this matter and the companies." Not only are there obvious grammatical errors here, it is also unclear what in the world the sender actually saw. Did the writer see many companies out there, or did he or she see the company's side of the matter? Who knows?

Whether employers like it or not, poor writing is not something to write off. Left unchecked, poor writing can cause performance and productivity to be off, too.

You get what you pay for

Q. I am thinking about giving my employees an attitude survey to learn more about what they like and dislike about working here. I found a free attitude survey on the Internet, and it looks pretty good to me. When I showed it to one of the managers, he was very critical of it. What should I be looking for in these surveys?

A. If you were to take a survey on employer attitudes regarding free surveys available on the Internet, you would probably find a good deal of dissatisfaction. Although these surveys might look attractive, especially from the price standpoint, there can be all sorts of problems associated with them.

The best surveys have questions that have been tested and validated, and that is quite foreign to most free surveys. Free surveys typically have questions that are poorly worded, and are often vague, ambiguous, or inappropriate. The scales for measuring such questions can also be a problem, especially those that try to insert some humor as part of the scale. Humor in a survey tends to make the process a joke.

Even if you find a great free questionnaire, that does not mean that you are home free. Administering the questionnaires is a science, in and of itself, and interpreting the findings and putting together a worthwhile action plan is even more critical.

A questionable survey not only generates useless data, but a good deal of dissatisfaction as well. As a result, perhaps the best thing to look for in an employee attitude survey is a professional firm to carry it out.

Monitors are monitored

Q. A good friend of mine is unemployed and called me at work and asked me to check out a job that he saw on the Internet. I went to the site, and just when I found it, my manager walked by my cubicle and saw it on the screen. I tried to explain, but I'm sure he thinks I'm looking for another job, which I am not. Should I talk to him further about what happened, or just let it go?

A. You mentioned that you tried to explain the matter to your manager, as opposed to saying that you did explain it to him. If you did not fully and clearly explain what happened here, you should do so.

Part of the problem is that employers today are concerned over the amount of time employees are spending online on sites that have nothing to do with work. Numerous employers are monitoring where the employees are going online, because the employees are on the company's equipment as well as on the company's payroll.

You need to make sure that your manager understands that you are not an employee who is online virtually all the time. Let him know the specifics of what happened here. Make it absolutely clear that you were trying to help a good friend who is out of work, but you recognize that you made a mistake. Wrap up the conversation with an apology.

The next step is to let the matter end here. You should let personal online pursuits end here, too.

Sighting too many sites

Q. My manager just told me that I have been spending too much time on golf sites on the Internet. I admit that I occasionally check out a couple of these sites, but I am more concerned that the company found out about this. Don't employees have some privacy?

A. You will find a lot more privacy on a golf course, which is where your employer would prefer you pursue your golfing links.

In many companies, employee privacy is rapidly evolving into an oxymoron. Increasing numbers of employers are not only monitoring employee Internet activity, but they are also checking out employee phone calls, e-mail, and general work habits. When employees come rolling into work, it is increasingly common to find that videotape starts rolling, too.

The rights of employees and employers in these areas are still evolving. If you are keeping score, the employers are definitely ahead.

From the employer standpoint, this monitoring is designed to focus on key work-related matters, such as maintaining quality work, preventing substance abuse, and identifying questionable performance. From the employee standpoint, this type of monitoring is typically viewed as being somewhere between an intrusion and an invasion.

The next time you consider visiting your favorite golf sites on company time and equipment, remember that there may be a gallery watching you. Your Website visits may help you shoot under par, but to the company they may be an indicator of a different kind of sub-par performance.

Chapter 19

Jerks on Cell Phones

It was not that many years ago that humans could actually survive a car ride to the local store or even to their offices without going into a state of panic because they did not have their cell phones. Those days are gone, and now most people cannot remember life before cell phones.

Cell phones have brought a long list of advantages to their users. On the productivity front, people can now conduct business from places that just a few years ago were totally commerce free, ranging from movie theatres to mountain tops. With cell phones, there is greatly increased access to employees, employers, vendors, and customers, as well as to any necessary emergency services. Those quiet bike rides, hikes, and strolls on the beach are now extra minutes or hours of productivity. In fact, it is difficult to conceive of venues where people cannot be accessed in a matter of seconds.

The power of cell phone technology has not gone unnoticed by jerks at work. Cell phones have given large cadres of jerks yet another opportunity to demonstrate the downside of even the most positive innovations. You do not have to look far to find people at the workplace who spend too much time on cell phones, interrupt their work and the work of others with so-called important calls, talk far too loud when on such calls, take and make calls in the most inappropriate places, and put themselves and those around them at risk when using the cell phone while driving, whether legal or not.

Although the thought of depositing their cell phones in the nearest dumpster is tantalizing indeed, you do not need to resort to such drastic measures. There are several less confrontational strategies that can put these cell phones and their users in their proper place.

Volume control

Q. We have many vendors stopping by throughout the week, and almost every day, there will be one who has a loud cell phone conversation. This interferes with our receptionist's work, and it is disturbing to other people in the waiting area as well. What's the best way to handle this?

A. There are increasing numbers of restrictions on cell phone usage in many sites, including automobiles, restaurants, theatres, and medical offices. The list is growing, and there is no reason why your waiting area should not be on it.

This does not mean that you confiscate the user's cell phone and cram it into the shredder, as tempting as that might be. Rather, all you need is a sign that politely asks visitors to please refrain from using their cell phone in the waiting area, and to handle all cell phone calls in the lobby or another appropriate exterior location.

It is particularly surprising to find that your vendors are doing this, because most vendors want to keep their customers happy, and this type of cell phone behavior does not do so.

Have you noticed the credo that many loud business cell phone calls seem to follow? The talker is typically waxing about some big deal, everyone else's mistakes, huge dollars, and the tons of money soon to arrive. You never hear the loud caller say, "I'm sorry," "My mistake," "Thanks, I learned a lot from this."

Either these loud callers are all perfect, or it's perfectly ridiculous to assume that these calls are necessary.

Up close and personal

Q. One of my employees seems to have many personal calls, but I am not sure. Whenever I walk into her office, she quickly hangs up. Sometimes it's her cell phone. If I ask about a call, she says it was business and got off quickly so I wouldn't have to wait. What do you think I should do?

A. Your employee's telephone antics sound phony. If you are on a business call and your manager walks into your office, do you instantly hang up? Hand gestures or briefly placing a call on hold are more normal reactions. Although you do not have ironclad evidence that she is on personal calls, her behavior is simply not what is found on business calls.

Although she is the one on the phone, part of the problem is your managerial style. Sometimes this type of thing happens with managers who are trying too hard to be liked.

Let your employee know that her actions certainly do not appear to be business calls, and then tell her where you and your company stand on this matter. Your company policy can be an excellent guide here, as employer rights can be rather broad in this area.

You should check up on her more often, document what you see and hear, and be sure she knows that if she continues this type of behavior, she is going to end up having a long-distance relationship with your company.

Driving you crazy

Q. I go to several business meetings each month with my manager, and he insists on driving. He is on the cell phone most of the time, and I cannot tell you how many times we have almost been in accidents. I asked him to either stop the calls or let me drive, but he won't. What do I do?

A. The practice of driving while using a cell phone has been outlawed in several states, while your manager remains in a state of denial. It sounds as though you have sat through enough close calls, whether on the road or on your manager's cell phone.

It is now time to do more than ask your manager to stop using the cell phone while he is driving. Because this practice is putting many lives in danger, you need to insist that you drive to these meetings.

Your manager may be more receptive if he can see the advantages associated with your taking the wheel. For example, he can devote more attention to the phone calls, avoid the hassles associated with traffic, and arrive at the destination feeling more refreshed and relaxed.

If he insists on hanging onto the steering wheel and the cell phone, tell him that you are going to drive your car to the meetings and will see him there. Because you are not having much conversation with him when you ride in his car, there is no need for you to be his passenger. The next time he checks his messages, hopefully he will get this important one from you.

Quite phony

Q. During an interview with an applicant for a sales job, his cell phone rang and he then took a brief business call. When it ended, he used the call as an example of his strong sense of customer service. How does this sound to you?

A. In a word, something about this call does not ring true. If a job applicant absolutely must take a cell phone call during an interview, he or she should advise the interviewer ahead that there is a particular situation that may cause this interruption. This type of call should be reserved for only the most urgent or critical communication. In such a context, the phone call is totally understandable.

As a rule, when a salesperson is meeting with a customer, that customer should be the center of the salesperson's attention. In your situation, as a potential employer, you were the customer and this applicant was a salesperson trying to sell his labor to you. It is a lapse in judgment for him to take a non emergency call while meeting with you. And his cavalier rationalization after the call did not help matters. One has to wonder if he is going to have these kinds of lapses in judgment if he is ultimately a salesperson for your company.

Being highly service-oriented is essential in successful selling today, but being honest, trustworthy, and credible is just as important. Perhaps that is why this individual did not sell you.

On hold, but not on a call

Q. I was meeting with one of the people who reports to me when her cell phone rang. She answered it and had a five-minute personal conversation, and then wanted to continue as if nothing had happened. I told her that if she ever did that again in a meeting with me, I would put a reprimand in her file. She thinks I overreacted, but I don't think so. Do you?

A. Overreacting in this case would have been to take her cell phone and stomp on it with the heel of your shoe. As it was, you were more than patient to hang around during her five-minute personal chat. In fact, it would have been altogether appropriate for you to walk out.

If your employee is in a meeting with you and receives an important business or personal call, whether on her cell phone or on a general business line, then she should say something to you about the call and continue after your approval. During the call, you should leave and continue your work, and the interrupted meeting will have to be rescheduled.

You have an employee who has no reluctance to take personal calls at work, probably in violation of company expectations or policy, and further, she has no reluctance to display her disregard for such standards right in front of you. In a word, you have to wonder what in the world is going through her mind.

Rather than being an isolated incident, this type of behavior is a critical incident that may point to other questionable workplace behaviors on her part. In a word, her personal call may actually be transmitting a very important message to you.

Say what?

Q. There is a new employee in our department who was spending huge amounts of time on personal calls. Our manager finally saw what she was up to and he told her to stop. Now she brings a cell phone and does the same thing, but claims it is her phone and she can make all the personal calls she wants. What do you think of this?

A. Your telephonic coworker is so far off the mark that she is in another area code. Although most employers do not want the employees using company phones for personal calls unless there is a real emergency, that was obviously not the message your manager was sending to your associate. Rather, the point was that when employees come to work, it would be nice if they spent their time working.

It is remarkable that your associate thinks that as long as she uses her own equipment, it is totally acceptable to chat all day. Under her assumption, although your company might not want employees sleeping at their desks, it would be permissible to zonk out all day if the employees bring a desk from home.

You and your associates can certainly tell your coworker that you need her help and would appreciate her spending less time on her cell phone and more time on her work. If she gives you static, then you should mention the problem to your manager. However, it sounds as though your manager is part of the problem itself. After all, if he were spending more time with the troops, your coworker would automatically be doing less dialing.

On the phone again

Q. I've been using a hand-held cell phone for years and have had no problems while driving. The other day my boss told me that I should get rid of it and use a hands-free unit or else pull over when I talk on the phone. I'll switch phones, but I'm really annoyed. Are many companies doing this?

A. Do not let yourself get hung-up over this development, as this type of change is being implemented in countless companies. While there is still debate over the extent that hand-held cell phones actually cause automobile accidents, there is no debate over the growing movement to eliminate their usage by drivers.

New York has a new law on the books that prohibits the use of such phones while driving, and at least 30 other states are considering similar legislation. At this point, ear microphones, headsets, and other hands-free options are allowed, but there is even talk about banning all dialing unless it is voice activated.

Your company is concerned about safety, not only in terms of its employees, but in terms of the general public as well. Obviously, your company is also concerned with the possible liabilities associated with accidents that occur when employees behind the wheel are more focused on steering a conversation than steering a car.

Switching to a hands-free option is an easy adjustment to make. Although you are annoyed about having to do so, it is a safe move to make in every respect.

The cell phone diet

Q. My boss is not the most accessible person in the world, and he has canceled many appointments with me. I got the bright idea to ask him to lunch, and he accepted. When we got to the restaurant, his cell phone rang and he took the call and several others after it. We probably had about five minutes of conversation the whole time. How do you deal with a boss such as this?

A. It's not particularly appetizing to take your boss to lunch so that he can catch up on communications with anyone but you. Looking at this behavior in combination with his prior cancellations of numerous appointments with you, it is apparent that he is sending several messages to you.

One inadvertent message is that he does not understand the importance of maintaining open communications with his employees. This can have a couple of different implications. On the one hand, he may believe that you are performing so well that you do not need much of his time. If this is the case, he is engaging in mismanagement because performance, motivation, and morale all tend to increase when employees have a good deal of two-way communication with their managers.

One the other hand he is not communicating with you because he is dissatisfied with your performance and does not want to take any further time with you. If this is the case, once again he is mismanaging. If an employee is struggling, it is particularly important to open the lines of communication with him or her, set a path of correction, and then communicate and coach along the way.

The fact is that you still need to have your meeting with your boss. One way to do so is to try the "drop-in" where you simply show up at his office during the day. If he cannot meet with you on the spot, try to nail down a time to meet later. Come back at that time, and although he may again defer the meeting, you may well get your meeting by the end of the day.

Another option is to invite him to lunch again. But this time, try to select a restaurant that does not allow the guests to use cell phones. If you cannot find one, simply pick a restaurant that you prefer, and if your manager takes a call on his cell phone, wait for him to hang up. As soon as he does, then take out your cell phone and call him. Maybe then he'll get your message. Bon appetit!

Chapter 20

Environ-Mental Impacts

There is no question that the work environment can have a significantly positive or negative impact on employee attitudes, satisfaction, and performance. At the same time, it is widely understood that even the most elaborate working conditions alone will not automatically lead to increased productivity.

Here's how this typically works: If the work environment is poorly designed, extremely hot, smelly, or physically disengaging for any other number of reasons, there is no way to effectively motivate the team. Their most basic needs are not being met in such settings, so these employees will not be energized by opportunities that might satisfy their higher level needs, such as opportunities for recognition, growth, or achievement.

However, once the harsh aspects of their work environments have been removed and replaced with more comfortable surroundings, the employees will still not necessarily be motivated. After all, there are plenty of beautiful offices that house totally sluggish employees. The bottom line is that environments do not motivate employees, but they can demotivate them.

If you want to motivate employees, the best way is to remove the harsh working conditions, try to understand your employees' individual needs, and then put together programs that align the fulfillment of these needs with attainment of work-related goals.

Unfortunately, the behavior and misbehavior of jerks can easily prevent any of this from happening. As you will see, instead of finding solutions to problems in the environment, today's jerks are going in the opposite direction and are turning environmental solutions into problems. Their antics undercut the workplace environment on matters as diverse and mundane as pets, plants, parking places, and paint. Based on the previous sentence, it almost sounds as though the jerks' negative impact is limited to instances that staart with the letter p. The truth is that they can disrupt the work environment from a to z.

The good news is that there are answers to the problems they cause, but they do need to be tackled before they start bringing the players down.

The office pet, literally

Q. I brought in a small fishbowl with a goldfish and put it on my desk. My manager told me that it has to go because company policy prohibits pets. I am in complete shock. It's just a tiny bowl with a fish in it. Should I take it home or stand up for what I think is right?

A. This might sound a little fishy, but many offices today have fish, whether in bowls, tanks, or even in ponds. There is a soothing, relaxing, and beautiful aspect to most fish. And further, feng shui, the ancient Chinese philosophy that focuses on spatial position and arrangement, holds that goldfish can bring good luck and prosperity, and that's not bad for the workplace either.

However, from your manager's perspective, you are violating a work rule. When companies turn their back on one rule, employees wonder if any of the rules truly need to be followed. And further, if you can bring in one goldfish, can another employee bring in 20, or even bring in more exotic fish with aerated 50-gallon tanks? Then, what about other pets? Can an employee bring in a cat? What happens when the cat spots the fish?

Although some companies allow certain pets at work and often find that they are a welcome addition, those are not your company. You should continue to discuss this matter with your manager and human resources department if there is one, but there is no point in making this a major battle. Surely you have more important fish to fry, so to speak.

Cramping your style

Q. I am in middle management and my office is small and cramped. Much of my work involves dealing with the public, and when people come to my office, I am embarrassed. Is it worth talking to my manager about this?

A. If the main problem with the size of your office is that you are embarrassed to work in such a tiny area, you will end up being even more embarrassed by bringing this up with your manager. The discussion will inevitably lead to the point that you should be spending more time thinking about your work and less time thinking about your work environment.

The only reason to approach your manager regarding a matter of this size is if your office is actually interfering with your productivity. For example, if people who visit you can hardly sit down, if there is no room to spread out important papers, or if people are getting injured by trying to angle themselves in and out of your office, then there is a legitimate reason to discuss this issue with your manager.

If there is nothing that either can or should be done with your office, it will be particularly important to remember that the most memorable part of your office is you. If you are embarrassed by the size of your office, your embarrassment is probably being noticed by those who visit you. However, your expertise, competence, and geniality can more than compensate for an office that doubles as a phone booth.

After all, there have been numerous sizable accomplishments emanating from miniscule offices. And conversely, there have been numerous miniscule accomplishments emanating from sizable offices.

Spaced out

Q. I was selected as employee of the month, and I was given a special parking place right in front of the building for one month. I came in one morning last week, and someone else was parked in it. When I complained, my manager said that I'm being petty and I should just find another place. What do you think of this treatment?

A. It does not sound as though your manager is in line to be manager of the month. He or she has taken a motivational program and totally undermined its meaning and effectiveness.

Unless there was a dire emergency, whoever owned the car should have been advised to move it. Short of that, you should be given an apology plus the place for an extra day.

When companies put in motivational programs and then fail to support them, all sorts of negative outcomes occur. For example, this type of treatment is demotivational not only to the impacted employee, but to his or her coworkers as well. People hear about what happened and they figure that it is simply not worth it to put forth the effort to become employee of the month.

In terms of the bigger picture, the company's credibility is undercut as well. The company made a commitment to the winning employee that he or she would have this special place, and then the company had no problem ignoring what it promised. If the company can't even be trusted in the parking lot, employees will wonder if it can be trusted anywhere.

A window of opportunity

Q. I am a manager, and our company is cutting back on office space. I just learned I am going to be working in an office with no windows. I think this is a step backward. I am upset and wonder if I should make an issue out of this.

A. When companies cut back, some employees lose a window and others lose a job. Although you are not happy with this development, you should take a look at the big picture and realize that although it is not a picture window, it is not all that terrible.

There are plenty of offices without windows that are still warm, inviting, and comfortable. You can find books and articles on this topic, and you may have a friend who can help with some plants, artwork, and layout ideas.

In these times, there are vast cadres of employees who have offices with spectacular views, but who has time to look? It is true that some status can be associated with having a window, but there are plenty of offices with windows and no employees at all.

You should not try to read too much into your move to a windowless office. The company has already demonstrated its faith in you. Your ability to hunker down and do a great job in this situation is going to give top management a revealing window into you.

Sculpting a problem

Q. The owner's wife just brought in a huge sculpture that she made for the waiting room. We all think it is obnoxious, but we are afraid to say so. Many clients have already made wisecracks about it, but we just smile politely. Should we say something to the owner or just forget about it?

A. If this huge sculpture is the biggest problem you literally face at work, consider yourself lucky. There are many employees out there who not only look at obnoxious creations but report to them.

If the owner's wife made this statue, and the owner likes it and presumably likes his wife, then the decision is pretty much cast in stone. The best step is to do just what you said and forget about it.

This statue is a recent change in the work environment, so it stands out in every respect. Given some time, changes in the foreground gradually move into the background, and you will ultimately give this statue about as much attention as you give to the noise being made by the air conditioning. Even the wisecracks from the clients are going to wind down over time.

The real risk down the road is if the owner's wife decides this statue needs a companion. Perhaps this is a good time to introduce her to the world of figurines.

The art of management

Q. My manager considers herself to be an artist, and she hung two of her paintings in her office. She asked me what I thought of them, and I sort of overstated my feelings, and now she wants me to buy one. I don't want one, but I don't want to upset her. How do I get out of this?

A. In your desire to be politically correct by giving rave reviews to your manager's paintings, you have painted yourself into a corner. This does not mean that you should have asked her if she had any trouble painting over the numbers, but tempered praise would have been adequate.

Obviously, your next step is not to buy a painting. You can tell her that you appreciate the offer and enjoy seeing the paintings on her walls, but at this point you are not in the market for this artwork. You can thank her again, but be sure that she understands that you are not a buyer. If she goes for the hard sell, or if you see repercussions down the road, you will need to have a more candid discussion with her, and with senior management if necessary.

The larger issue is that your manager has absolutely no business turning her office into an arts and crafts bazaar. She is probably in violation of company policy on this one, as her actions waste time, generate stress, and interfere with the ability of staff to meet departmental objectives. Senior management will not view this as an effective display of the art of management. In fact, managers who hustle the employees are often hustled out the door.

A pointed discussion

Q. I just brought a fairly large cactus into my office, and the office manager caught sight of it and said that it is not an appropriate plant for an office. She said that it gives off a threatening atmosphere and the thorns pose a safety risk, so, it has to go. Have you ever heard of such a thing?

A. Of all the growing issues that one encounters at work, it is initially surprising to find that your office manager wants to handle a cactus. Your office manager is stuck on two points, but only one holds water.

Saying that a cactus poses a threatening atmosphere throws an unwarranted barb at the plant itself. Cacti are among the most beautiful, intriguing, and inviting plants in the world. Besides, with a number of states experiencing a drought right now, a cactus might just be the perfect plant.

However, the one thorny issue is what constitutes "fairly large." If your cactus overpowers the office and threatens to puncture any who dare to enter, then your office manager does have a basis for some concern.

You should discuss the situation with your office manager and see if there is any wiggle room, not only on this matter but in your office as well. Importantly, this is not an issue that calls for a major battle. If the plant is deemed unacceptable, then it has to hit the road. Perhaps you can replace it with something else, such as a rose bush.

Don't mess up with your boss

Q. My office is a mess. I have piles of work scattered all over the place, but I know where everything is. I can find what I need quickly, even if I have to step over a pile or two. My boss said this is unacceptable and I have to clean it up. Does this make sense to you?

A. Your office may be a mess, but you can get into an even bigger mess if you decide to go to battle with your boss over this request. On one level, if you are performing well, the fact that your office is a hovel should not matter a great deal.

However, there are circumstances where the cleanliness and orderliness of your office can make a difference. For example, you said that you occasionally have to step over a pile or two. That instantly points to a safety problem and the increased likelihood of someone tripping and falling when navigating in your office, and that someone can easily be you.

Although you claim that you can quickly access whatever you need, you would be able to do so quicker if your office were well-organized. This obviously does not mean cramming a bunch of files into a cabinet and then shoving the drawers closed. There are real systems to help you organize your work, and there is even a question as to why you have so many piles of paper in this increasingly paperless world of work.

By getting things in order, you will be able to find what you need even faster, and you will reduce the likelihood of doing so by accident.

Children's masterpieces

Q. My boss just told me that I have too much of my children's artwork in my office, and I should take some of it down. I don't want to remove it. Having their work around me makes me feel good, and my children love it when they visit. How would you suggest I handle this?

A. When dealing with children's artwork in an office, it is important to avoid having so much art that there is no room for work. On the one hand, it is important for your manager to focus on the big picture rather than on the children's pictures. Most employees put some personal touches in their offices, and employers are typically glad that they do so. At the same time, having your children's artwork in your office can mean having a few of their strategically-placed artistic creations, or it can mean that your office resembles a preschool classroom at the end of a rainy week.

At this point, you should literally and figuratively step back and take a look at your office. If your children's creations are in no way interfering with your work, accessibility, concentration, or dealings with the rest of the staff, that is what you should tell your manager. Let him know that having all of this artwork actually contributes to your satisfaction and productivity. He is not likely to insist that you remove something that makes you more effective on the job.

At the same time, when it comes to decorating, there is truth to the adage that less is more. If you see some areas where the collection could be thinned out a bit, it would probably be an artful move to do so.

Extremely casual attire

Q. I am a department manager in an organization that allows the employees to "dress down" on Fridays. There is no written policy in this area, and many employees are wearing clothes that are inappropriate for work. Lately some of our customers have made comments. How do I deal with this?

A. When employees are told that they can "dress down," and the guidelines are vague at best, the employees will dress down...in many cases, way down. And further, the attire will continue its descent unless some action is taken.

Programs that allow the employees to dress comfortably for work can be very helpful in improving morale, satisfaction, and even productivity. While it is not critical to have a written policy in this area, it is essential to have widely-shared agreement as to what is and is not appropriate. The best way to reach this understanding is through direct communication.

The first step is to openly and honestly tell the employees that the current level of attire on Fridays has dipped into the unacceptable range, and customers are commenting about it. Give them specific information regarding the kinds of attire that have generated complaints or other work-related problems, as well as a clearer picture of the kinds of attire that are acceptable. Let the employees know that you view them as adults and expect them to make reasonable individual decisions as to what they should be wearing to work on the free-dress days.

In the event that some employees still do not get the message, the next step is to develop a more formalized standard. While you could do this on your own, it will be more effective to form a task force of key employees to suggest some guidelines. By having employee involvement at this stage of the process, you increase the likelihood of having a quality program that is actually followed.

While not a major issue, one change that should be considered is the name of the program. The term, "dress down," can send a psychological message that attire is expected to sink to greater and greater depths—in fact, it is almost a subtle directive to do so. As a result, it will make more sense to use words such as "casual" or "comfortable" in referring to attire for the special days.

A moving experience

Q. When I returned from a short vacation, I found that my office had been moved from one part of the building to another. I never had been told about this, and no one else's office was moved. I am furious. I told my manager and he said that it just needed to be done. Does this sound right to you?

A. There can be some good reasons for management to move an employee's office when the employee is not present, but most are related to disasters such as earthquakes, fires, or monsoons. When management unilaterally moves an employee's office under most other circumstances, it simply causes a disaster.

Even if your manager is somehow correct and your office just needed to be moved, whatever that means, there still should have been communication with you regarding this prospect.

Looking at the bigger picture, you need to ask yourself if this kind of treatment is typical of the way that your company is run. If this is some sort of an aberration, it will be important for senior management to understand your dissatisfaction with the process, as well as your desire to be directly involved in any such decisions in the future. Again, if this moving experience is typical of the way that things are done in your company, you need to decide if you can live with this managerial style, or if it is time for you to move.

Chapter 21

When Jerks Push the Envelope

This final chapter is designed to give you an idea of the kinds of behaviors that jerks at work can display when they are turned completely loose, with no restraints, compunctions, boundaries, or barriers. These real-world jerks have engaged in workplace behaviors that are guaranteed to stun you. Their actions, practices, policies, and decisions truly qualify as consummate jerk behaviors.

While there are answers to every question, reinforced with specific steps and strategies, you are still going to be left with one question after reading them: What in the world were these jerks thinking?

Hopefully you will be able to sit back and say that these behaviors are so outrageous that no one would ever do anything like this where you work. However, if you stop for a minute and think about some of the jerks who are bouncing around your workplace right now, you might just think of one or two who are quite capable of reaching these low marks.

So, here they are: Out of all of the letters submitted to my syndicated column during the more than five past years, a sampling of 12 of the most outrageous, ridiculous, and counterproductive behaviors by jerks at work.

Don't be accommodating

Q. When we travel to trade shows for our company, we are expected to share accommodations with other employees of the company. Sometimes these accommodations are coed. Is this proper etiquette for our company to expect the employees to share and what should the guidelines be?

A. This brings to mind an image of a management meeting where some topsider says, "Can we come up with an outrageous policy that will upset the employees, invade their privacy, and maybe get us sued?" After a moment of silence, one manager in the back of the room jumps up and says, "I've got it! Coed rooms on business trips!" With resounding cheers and backslapping, the meeting adjourns.

As to whether it is proper etiquette to expect the employees to share coed rooms, the answer is, no! In addition, it is not a proper policy, it is not proper ethics, and it is not proper management. It is not proper, period. Management needs to be advised of this fact and told that although they are interested in cutting costs, there are tremendous costs associated with this policy.

As for some guidelines in this type of business situation, there are companies that will place employees of the same sex in the same hotel rooms. However, even in this type of scenario, the employees are often given the opportunity to voice some preferences.

Just because your company is sending you to a trade show does not mean that you have to trade your privacy, values, and sense of what's right and wrong.

You wore what?

Q. I work in a well-known apparel company and I wore a shirt that had the logo from one of our competitors. I did it because I like the shirt, not because I was trying to make a joke or some kind of statement. My boss was furious, and so were several other managers. I won't do it again, but I could not believe how insecure they were about this. Is this really that big of a deal?

A. Showing up at work and basically sporting an advertisement for the competition is simply asking for trouble. Here is an easy way to look at this: many companies envision themselves as teams, and you showed up wearing an opponent's jersey. What would happen to a member of the New York Yankees who showed up for a game wearing a Boston Red Sox jersey?

You mentioned this was not a joke, but perhaps you could have gotten away with this if it were some sort of joke. By thinking that your behavior was not a big deal, you have inadvertently sent a message that points to a lack of understanding of the business and industry, disloyalty to the company, lack of pride in the company, insensitivity to your fellow employees, and real questions about your judgment.

You also mentioned that management's reaction is a sign of insecurity, but all that has happened is that you have undermined your own job security. Employers prefer employees who would give them the shirts off their backs, and that's exactly what you should do in all respects.

Manager in name only

Q. I have an East European name, and one of the managers here makes fun of it, often asking if he can "buy a vowel." I have a sense of humor, but I am tired of hearing this from him and I have told him to stop. He keeps doing it and says he means no harm and is just having fun. How do I get him to stop?

A. If your manager persists with his so-called fun, perhaps he should think about buying a vowel for this word: L_WSUIT. Regardless of his intent, his hurtful comments smack of discrimination based on national origin, and that's just asking to get smacked with litigation.

It is rather amazing that there are still people around who make comments such as this. Those who do so must either live under a huge rock, or they are unbelievably insensitive, uniformed, self-absorbed, or misguided, or a combination of all of these delightful characteristics.

You should deal directly and firmly with this individual. Tell him that you find his comments to be cruel and hurtful, and then add that they have to stop immediately. End the discussion by telling him that you hope you do not have to take any further action on this matter, but you will if you must. If he still does not get the message, then you should deliver it to his manager.

Plant management

Q. I am in management, and the managers' offices have plants, and all are thriving but mine. After a recent meeting in my office, my manager suggested that my attitude might be causing the plants to do poorly. I thought he was kidding, but he wasn't. And I don't have a negative attitude. What should I say to him?

A. There are plenty of outrageously inept, dissatisfied, and negative managers whose offices have more lush greenery than a rain forest. For your manager to even hint that your attitude is killing the foliage in your office means that your plant is actually evaluating your performance, an approach that sits somewhere near the top of the ridiculous scale.

Now, there are people who say that if you want plants to thrive, you should be nice to them and talk to them. That of course explains why so many plants thrive on the freeways and turnpikes directly adjacent to semi-trucks, honking horns, exhaust fumes, and discarded garbage.

The only useful piece of data in this encounter with your manager is that he thinks you have a negative attitude. You should dig further into this assertion, starting with an honest self-assessment. You should then meet with your manager.

It will be important to emphasize the fact that the best measures of your attitude are your performance, productivity, and ability to inspire and motivate those around you. Try to bring some hard performance data that reflect your attitude, efforts, leadership, and drive.

Your attitude has nothing to do with your ability to inspire your plants to bloom, but it has a great deal to do with your ability to inspire your employees to bloom.

Under the knife

Q. I am a 55-year-old female, and I heard that I would have a better chance of getting a job if I looked younger. I am considering having some minor surgery, and I was wondering if you think that doing so actually helps make someone more marketable.

A. There are plenty of young people looking for work in the current flooded labor market, and it is entirely possible that you could go through a whole surgical ordeal, only to look like an unemployed younger person instead of an unemployed baby boomer. Realistically, if the operation is a major success, you may look younger, but you are not going to be mistaken for a Generation X'er.

As a result of the surgery, you may feel better about yourself, and that can help you project more confidence in the interview. In such a scenario, perhaps your change of face may change your prospects of landing a job.

However, you are still talking about an operation, and there are no guarantees of anything. Before spending time and money on surgery, you should also consider spending it on something that may not change your appearance, but may well change your performance, namely education. Your chances of having an employer give you a second glance are often greater if your leadership and technical skills, rather than your face, are at the cutting edge.

Pseudo psychology

Q. When I sit at my desk, I usually tuck one leg under the other. One of the senior consultants said that a personality test on the Internet found that when a male sits like this, it is a sign of deference and weakness. He added that I should never do it in front of a client. Did you ever hear of anything such as this?

A. It must have been difficult for you to sit through this senior consultant's inane comments. Telling people how to live their lives as a result of pseudo-psychological tests on the Internet is not exactly state-of-the-art management.

The Internet is a great dumping ground for would-be psychological tests from never-would-be psychologists. These tests can be packaged with appropriate lingo, but they lack the in-depth analysis and validation that accompanies all professional psychological tests.

While many aspects of body language can be quite revealing, such as a person's facial expression and certain gestures, crossing one leg under the other simply does not fall into the category of personality indicators. The main reason why you sit with your legs in such a position is that it is comfortable for you.

If your manager is truly interested in making an accurate judgment about your deference or strength, there is something that can give him far more accurate insight. It's called your behavior. Drawing conclusions about personality on the basis of simple tests on the Internet is virtually absurd.

Sports talk

Q. I know it's popular to use sports language when managing, but our boss has gone to an extreme. We're always going to the hoop, trying to hit more home runs, or looking for the slam dunk. Yesterday he gave me one of his sports talks and then patted me on the rear. I told him to never do that again. Any suggestions on how to deal with him?

A. Using your manager's terminology, patting an employee on the rear is an illegal use of the hands. And, there's a huge penalty for that type of conduct.

Although many managers today are using sports comments as a seemingly colorful and creative way to communicate, this approach can miss the individual needs of many of the employees. Simply put, sports talk is not for everyone.

The larger problem with your manager is that he is not only unaware of the impact that his language and style are having on you and your associates, he is also unaware of at least one very basic issue at work these days, namely unwanted touching. And that's probably not the only issue that is missing from his playbook.

You and some of your associates should see if he would be willing to discuss ways to help the department run more effectively. In the context of such a discussion, he could be told that some of the employees do not respond particularly well to comments laced with sports references. A few sharp words about the issue of sexual harassment are in order as well. He needs to understand that there is more to management than fun and games.

Oooooops

Q. I sent an e-mail to one of my close friends here, and I included some fairly nasty comments about some of the people here, including our manager. The problem is that I must have hit the wrong button because it went to just about everybody. Obviously a lot of people are very upset with me. What can I do?

A. Other than update your resume, your best hope is to offer apologies to all of the people that you slammed. Do this individually with each of them, including your manager, and then see what happens.

While the specific comments that you included in the e-mail play a role here, the greater problem is that your credibility, judgment, and loyalty have all fallen into serious doubt. Many employees are going to wonder if they can trust you, and others may distance themselves from you because you insulted them or because you are politically on the outs.

There are times when an employee makes such a major error that he or she cannot continue with the firm. Sometimes this outcome is evident immediately, while in other situations it can take a little while. The fact that you are still at the company indicates that the jury is still out.

During this time, try to put the matter behind you and demonstrate not only your diligence but the fact that you learned something. The reaction of your manager and fellow employees will let you know if they want to teach you another lesson.

What are you waiting for?

Q. A year ago, my boss hired "Joe" to help me with my workload. Joe gets along well with the boss, but everyone else in the office is afraid of him. He has a violent temper and swears constantly. When someone talks nicely to him, he'll make a violent threat such as, "How about I smash your head in with a sledgehammer?" I told my boss that we don't feel safe with Joe working here, but he refuses to do anything. In fact, he thinks the whole situation is funny. Should I search for a job elsewhere before Joe gets totally out of hand?

A. It sounds as though "Joe" is literally and figuratively a loose cannon, and it is outrageous that your boss somehow thinks that his threat to harm someone with a sledgehammer is funny. Every threat is deadly serious. You need to take immediate action to deal with this matter.

You and your associates should bypass your boss and go directly to the most senior level person you can access in your company and describe what is happening. Companies have a legal obligation to provide a safe work environment, and there is already major exposure because your boss has been advised of the problem. Someone in a topside position needs to investigate this matter right now. Threatening an employee with bodily harm warrants immediate and severe managerial action.

You may indeed wish to change jobs, but if management takes swift action on this matter, you need not rush the decision. The only rush is to make sure that you and your associates are safe.

There's trouble afoot

Q. I was at a meeting with my manager and some members of senior management, and whenever I talked, my manager kicked me. I didn't know if he wanted me to keep talking or be quiet, so I ignored him. After the meeting, he said I was talking too much, and he was kicking me to get me to stop. I am annoyed and don't know what to what tell him.

A. In the parlance of body language, a kick generally means for people to stop and mules to go. However, a manager is acting like mule if he is kicking employees during a meeting. But if an employee is galloping down the wrong path in a meeting, some managers feel that the only way to rein things in is with a boot.

This means that you should look at your behavior as well as that of your manager. On the one hand, is it possible that you may have been a little too verbal? On the other hand, is it possible that you and your manager were ill-prepared? If a manager has worked with his or her staff and anticipated the questions, issues, and concerns that may arise in a meeting, the likelihood of an employee heading in the wrong direction is dramatically decreased.

Either way, you should tell your manager that you absolutely do not want to be kicked or touched in any way by him again. Unless he gets his kicks by increasing legal exposure for himself and the company, he should be smart enough to pull the reins on this behavior.

Bikes and biases

Q. I recently hired a store manager, and I just learned that she rides a motorcycle to work. I don't think this is the right image for our company, and I am concerned about the example she may be setting for the rest of the staff. When she came to the interview, she arrived in a car, and this issue never came up. How do I approach it now?

A. As it is, you are approaching this employee in the slow lane, and the best advice is to take the next off ramp. If this employee is getting to work on time and in condition to fully execute all of her responsibilities, whether she arrives on roller blades, a pogo stick, or a llama is not your concern.

If there are specific work-related problems that are somehow being caused by her mode of transportation, you should discuss such matters with her. However, even if she looks as though she stepped out of a wind tunnel, which she probably does not, there is no reason to assume that this appearance would be detrimental to her performance.

It sounds as though her motorcycling has driven into some of your biases and stereotypes, not only regarding motorcycles, but regarding females as well. The fact is that her mode of transportation could just as easily be telling you that she is independent, enjoys the outdoors, cares about conserving energy, and is not one to complain about the lack of parking for employees.

Although you expressed concern about the corporate image and the example being set, it is possible that this managers "approach" to work may do wonders in both of these areas.

Giving a toast versus becoming toast

Q. We had our company holiday party yesterday, and I drank more than usual. I had sort of a good time, but I know I was too loud, and I almost passed out. My friend who drove me home told me that my manager noticed and did not look pleased. What should I do now? Apologize or just let it go?

A. When you drink to the point that you almost passed out at the company holiday party, you literally need to step back and smell the coffee. You are not only endangering your career, you are putting everything and everyone else at risk as well.

Should you talk to your manager about what happened here? The answer is yes. He or she may well be wondering about your judgment, maturity, professionalism, and potential. Your manager may also be concerned about your health. You should be prepared with an explanation, apology, and commitment to take action to prevent this from happening again.

It is also time for an honest self-evaluation. Perhaps your actions were an aberration or a lapse in judgment, and hopefully you learned from this mistake. However, is it possible that there is something else going on here that needs professional attention? Your company may have an employee assistance program to help you answer this.

Either way, it is important to see these year-end gatherings for what they really are. A company holiday party is a company party, not a holiday party. When an employee almost passes out at one, employers tend to remember this when they pass out promotions, raises, and choice projects.

Conclusion

My objective in writing a revised edition of *Jerks at Work* has been to take a look at the newest kinds of behaviors that jerks are displaying in the workplace and provide you with the newest tools and strategies to deal with them.

As in the past, in order to deal effectively with card-carrying jerks and the real-life problems they create, it is still critical to look not only at their behavior, but also try to glean some kind of understanding of what makes them tick. By looking at these individuals in this light, you will be able to shed more light on how to deal with them. At the same time, by drawing on state-of-the-art research in areas as diverse as pediatrics, management, and sociology, my hope is to provide you with some new paths to deal with people problems and problem people.

However, there is no instant strategy that automatically applies to all jerks at work. Some of their antics call for swift, direct, and assertive action, lest matters quickly spiral out of control. In other cases, their antics call for a more measured approach and the use of more analysis, patience, and persuasion. However, in no case does it make sense to simply ignore the behavior of jerks at work—ironically enough, that is just what a jerk would do.

And speaking of avoiding jerk-like behaviors, it is still true that many people actually learn how to become jerks at work by emulating the behavior of their managers and fellow employees. In fact, studies have found that the behavior of new managers is remarkably close to the behavior of their own managers, especially their first managers. This means that all of us are models in our workplace, and if we act like jerks, we should expect those who work with us to do the same.

This raises the question of how to be a positive role model as opposed to being a model jerk at work. Here are some steps to help meet this objective:

+ Treat people with respect and trust.
+ Try to understand others as individuals.
+ Remember that people are an organization's most valuable resources.
+ Treat all of your team as customers.
+ Listen to what others have to say.
+ Manage by wandering around.
+ Be accessible, open, and responsive to your associates and team.
+ Be fair, honest, and ethical.
+ Recognize the value of diversity.
+ Keep the lines of communication open.
+ Be a team player.
+ Read voraciously about your field, and read some fiction, too.
+ Take classes in and out of your area of expertise.
+ Encourage employee training, development, and education.
+ Jointly establish realistic goals and plans.
+ Look for solutions, not just problems.
+ Set positive expectations.
+ Give thanks and recognition when due.
+ Keep quality and service clearly in mind.

+ Encourage and reward creative and innovative thinking.
+ And most importantly, remember that only a jerk ignores the Golden Rule.

My final hope is that this book has provided you with additional insights and tools to help you understand, handle, and possibly prevent jerk behaviors by your managers, coworkers, employees, customers, vendors, and most importantly, by you.

If you have further questions or need an extra edge in dealing with jerks at work or other people-related issues or problems on the job, you can contact me online through my column at either nytsyn-lloyd@nytimes.com or LloydOnJob@aol.com, or you can send me a letter at P.O. Box 260057, Encino, CA 91426. There is also a broad range of additional information and resources available to you at *jerksatwork.com.*

Index

About the Author

Ken Lloyd, Ph.D., is a nationally recognized consultant, author, educator, and newspaper columnist based in Encino, California. With specialties in organizational behavior, management training and development, and communication, Dr. Lloyd has consulted in a wide range of industries including healthcare, apparel, financial services, electronics, Internet service provider, and entertainment. His nationally syndicated workplace advice column (*New York Times* Syndicate) appears in newspapers across the United States.

He is the author of the widely acclaimed *Jerks at Work: How to Deal With People Problems and Problem People* (Career Press, 1999), available in numerous languages including Chinese, Japanese, and Korean. He also authored, *Be the Boss Your Employees Deserve* (Career Press, 2002), and co-authored, *Ultimate Selling Power: How to Create and Enjoy a Multi-million Dollar Sales Career* (Career Press/Penguin Books, 2002), along with the best selling book, *Unlimited Selling Power: How to Master Hypnotic Selling Skills* (Prentice Hall, 1990), now in its ninth printing and available in numerous languages. Dr. Lloyd is also the author of, *The K.I.S.S. Guide to Selling* (DK Publishers, 2001), part of Dorling Kindersley's popular "Keep It Simple Series."

Dr. Lloyd is a frequent television and talk-radio guest, and he has appeared on *Good Morning America*, CNN, Morning Edition on NPR, along with several appearances on KABC, Fox Morning News, and KTLA in Los Angeles. He received his B.A. from UC Berkeley, and his Ph.D. in Organizational Behavior from UCLA. He teaches frequently in the MBA Program at the Anderson Graduate School of Management at UCLA, and he continues to lecture at various universities and speak before numerous organizations and associations. Dr. Lloyd is a member of the American Psychological Association and the Society for Industrial and Organizational Psychology.